THE FORTY-NINERS

Books by Linda Pendleton

Fiction:
The Unknown, A Novel
Corn Silk Days, Iowa, 1862
Sound of Silence
Shattered Lens: Catherine Winter, Private Investigator
Fractured Image: Catherine Winter, Private Investigator
The Masquerading Cowboy (A Novella)
Roulette: The Search for the Sunrise Killer by Don and Linda
Pendleton

Nonfiction:
Three Principles of Angelic Wisdom
A Walk Through Grief
A Small Drop of Ink
To Dance With Angels by Don and Linda Pendleton
Whispers From the Soul by Don and Linda Pendleton
Metaphysics of the Novel by Don Pendleton, Linda Pendleton

Comic Adaptations:
The Executioner War Against the Mafia, Don and Linda
Pendleton
The Executioner Death Squad, Linda Pendleton

THE FORTY-NINERS

The California Gold Rush

Stewart Edward White

Introduction by Linda Pendleton

Pendleton Artists
California

ISBN-13: 978-1470103613
ISBN-10: 1470103613

The Forty-niners, was originally published in the United States,
1918, by Steward Edward White. Public Domain.

Print Edition, 2012.
Kindle Edition by Pendleton Artists, April, 2010
Cover Design by Judy Bullard

Pendleton Artists
California

www.lindapendleton.com

Printed and bound in the United States of America
by
Create Space
100 Enterprise Way
Suite A 200
Scotts Valley, CA 95066

Contents

Introduction by Linda Pendleton

More than one hundred years ago, Stewart Edward White became a writer. He was a lover of nature: an explorer, conservationist, naturalist, and big game hunter. His love for nature, conservation, and adventure were to become very much a part of his literary works over his long career. Stewart once said his books, including his novels, were stories based upon actual experience. He loved writing about pioneers, the West, logging, and nature.

Born in Grand Rapids, Michigan, March 12, 1873, to Thomas Stewart White and Mary Daniell White, he was educated at the University of Michigan and received a Master of Arts Degree in 1903 from Columbia University. His father, Thomas, a successful lumberman, who owned a number of mills in the Grand Rapids area and then in later years in California, was an active outdoorsman and introduced his sons to nature, camping, hunting, and hiking, giving Stewart his passion for these interests. Thomas White was a very successful mill owner and his company White and Friant, ran all the logs in the river at Grand Rapids to Grand Haven, booming, sorting, and delivering them to mills along the way. In later years, one of his companies milled Sugar Pine in California.

There were five White sons, and while Stewart would become a writer, his brother, Thomas Gilbert White (1877), would become a world renowned artist, known for his murals. During World War I, Thomas Gilbert White became a decorated member of the United States Army Reserves. He lived in Paris, France and studied with well known artists Jean Paul Laurens, Benjamin Constant, and James McNeil Whistler. He would paint the commissioned murals in Paris and ship them to the United States. Several are in state capitol buildings in Utah and Kentucky as well as the Agricultural Building in Washington D.C. One well-known work, at the Oklahoma State Capitol, *Pro Patria*, was commissioned by Bartlesville Oklahoma oilman Frank Phillips to commemorate the tragedies and triumphs of World War I. The central panel represents the courage and sacrifice of a brave soldier answering his country's call to war. The right and left panels honor fallen soldiers. Thomas Gilbert White painted the massive mural in his Paris studio and meticulously added the names of the 2,735 Oklahoma soldiers who died during WW I.

The White Mural was dedicated Armistice Day, November 11, 1928; the Capitol Rotunda was filled to capacity. At the dedication, Thomas Gilbert White declared, "through these canvases, may the muffled voices from the grave speak to the generations to come of a day when men were not too proud to fight and held life less than their country's honor."

Thomas Gilbert White's work can be found among the permanent collections of the Corcoran, the Brooklyn Museum, the Philadelphia Museum of Art and the City of Paris Museum.

Another talented brother was Roderick White (1890), who became a world-touring violinist, studying internationally, and playing in Germany's Dresden Royal Opera House in 1913.

Stewart's brother, Harwood Arend White (1896), a graduate of Princeton, and an Air Force veteran of World War I, was a professional tennis coach for many years at the Montecito Country Club in Santa Barbara, California. He authored books on tennis, and collaborated on the nonfiction book, *Across the Unknown*, with his brother Stewart.

And further, brother, Rugee White, would carry on White and Friant Company, the family lumber business in Grand Rapids, Michigan.

While still a young man in his teens, Stewart and brother, Thomas Gilbert White, studied the birds of their home state of Michigan, and wrote and illustrated articles on birds that were used by the University of Michigan. In 1907, the University considered the young brothers to be "leading authorities on the subject." He was honored by the American Association for the Advancement of Science for his writings on bird life.

Stewart's first book, *The Westerner* was published in 1901. He was twenty-eight years of age. That was the beginning of his successful literary career and he would go on to publish more than 50 books and short stories, including Westerns, pioneer and adventure stories, children stories, and nonfiction over his career that lasted until his death, September 18, 1946 in Hillsborough, California.

Stewart once said his books were stories based upon actual experience. He loved writing about pioneers, the West, logging, and nature, and time spent around logging, milling, and even gold mining, enriched his stories. Two of his novels, *The Blazed Trail* (1902) and the *Riverman (1908)* were about logging in Michigan.

By 1903, the family had moved to Santa Barbara, California, and in April, 1904, Stewart married Elizabeth (Betty) Calvert Grant and they made their home in Santa Barbara for a few years. Following their marriage their unique honeymoon was spent camping in the Sierra Nevada Mountains of California. From their wedding journey came a series of articles by White, published in *Outlook Magazine,* and then published as the book, *The Mountains,* later in 1904. Several of his books were not only melodramatic Westerns but also autobiographical. It was said that Stewart Edward White knew the lands of which he wrote. When he talked of his schooling in his formative years and university studies, he said, "During those years I was more in the woods and on the water than in school." He added, "However I was graduated."

An early article about him not long after *The Westerners* was published, stated, "Since graduation Mr. White has passed much of his time in cattle, mining and forest regions of this country, with intervening periods of Eastern residence and European travel. This summer he is off on a long exploring tour of the Hudson Bay region. Thus, we see, Stewart Edward White knows the land of which he writes. He has ridden on its plains and ranches, has explored its wildernesses, has hunted in its forests, and has prospected in its mining camps. He has lived with the men of the Far West, as they were in their most interesting stages of its development—the cowboy, the prospector, the miner, the woodsman, the riverman—yes, and appreciates the part which they have played in the construction of a tremendous economic power. It is Mr. White's intention to write a series of thoroughly American novels dealing with material which has been left untouched in this land of riches."

Several of his works became movies or miniseries. *Conjurer's House*, published in 1909, first became a play and story adapted by George Broadhurst and in August of 1914 was a silent film, directed and produced by Cecil B. De Mille. It was De Mille's second directing credit. In 1921, *Conjurer's House*, an adventure drama, was filmed on location in the Big Bear Lake area of Southern California, as *The Call of the North*.

His 1919 novel, *The Killer*, was adapted to film in 1932 as *Mystery Ranch*. In the late 1950s his stories of *The Saga of Andy Burnett* were made into a Disney miniseries for television. The story was based on four of White's books about a young boy who leaves home with a rifle that once belonged to Daniel Boone and heads West, the first of the book series being published in 1932.

In 1911, Stewart went on an African adventure and he wrote to his publisher that he was "having bully time on his African expedition; has shot thirty-nine different species of game, including seven lions, and has been in some really tight squeaks."

March 6, 1925, Stewart's left the port of New York for Africa with Drs. Saxton T. Pope and Arthur Young. White said they expected to be gone eight or nine months. Before he left he was quoted as saying, "I have shot thirty-seven lions and two elephants, but this will be my first trial with the bow and arrow. I feel like a novice at this new method of hunting, compared with my colleague, Dr. Pope, who has used it for eight or nine years....Hunting with a bow and arrow is more sport than with the rifle, and it is also more humane."

Although White was a big game hunter, he denounced hunting down a leopard with gunpowder. *Time Magazine* reported June 29, 1925, a story of a leopard and the challenge it gave White and his two hunting natives. I quote from it:

"Deep in the African jungle, the natives halted sharply, stiffened, passed the word. A leopard. Stalking began. Stewart Edward White was in the lead, in his hands a bow cut from the sturdy yew trees of California. The bow string was the length of the old cloth yard—27 ½ in., and it took 80 pounds of pulling power, and much skill to draw one of the 5 ½ ft. steel-tipped arrows, also of yew, to the head of the bow. It was a clumsy thing, this bow, difficult to keep clear of the jungle undergrowth, not a thing to discharge instantaneous death in a second into a springing leopard. The leopard was a good 100 ft. away. It was a long shot. White made it."

Don't you just love that visual description? Can't you see the curve of the bow?—One of the arrows nearly as tall as White?—The black leopard ready to spring into action? Now, Steward Edward White was not a big man at all. Descriptions I have read have him on the slim side and not an exceptionally tall man.

The article goes on to say that the leopard dropped but then the leopard surprised one of the natives and clawed him. The other native who carried a gun fired and the leopard reacted again and bit the man. White managed to fire a second shot but the leopard then attacked him, biting him in the shoulder. White was able to sink his hunting knife into the leopard, killing it.

When asked if hunting with gunpowder was justice and sportsmanship, White said, "No, it is not sportsmanship; it is disgraceful butchery. For my part, I am going to give the lion and the tiger a sporting chance. I shall hunt them with the bow and arrow."

During World War I, White enlisted and served in the 144th Field Artillery and achieved the rank of major. He was made a fellow of the Royal Geographic Society of London after mapping German East Africa in 1913.

Apparently White and Col. Theodore Roosevelt (later to become President Roosevelt) not only shared big game hunting but the appreciation for the ecology and conservationism. President Theodore Roosevelt wrote an article against a Dr. William J. Long, in regards to what the President called *nature fakers* and irresponsible people in regards to giving false information about wolves. He lists White as one of six naturalists to whom "we owe a real debt."

When the Federal Fishery Bureau discovered new varieties of Rainbow Trout in the High Sierra Mountains of California, the two new varieties of the Golden trout were named after Theodore Roosevelt and Stewart Edward White.

A subspecies of the Rainbow trout, the Golden trout of the Little Kern River (California), the *O. m. Whitei*, was named after Stewart Edward White, who in 1904 wrote the book, *The Mountains.* He thereafter urged President Theodore Roosevelt to send an expedition to study the Golden trout in its habitat and to assure that hatchery fish would not destroy the natural Golden trout of the area.

White's suggestion was apparently not heeded, and in May 15, 1978, the Little Kern River native Golden trout (referred to as: *salmo aguabonita whitei*) was designated as Threatened and added to the Federal Endangered and Threatened Species list.

In 1955, a grove of Sequoia trees at Prairie Creek Redwood State Park along the Northern California coastal area, was named after Stewart Edward White.

In September, 1909, an expedition to San Clemente Island off the Pacific coast near Santa Barbara almost ended in tragedy. White was accompanied by United States Senator from California, Frank Putman Flint, Gifford Pinchot, United States Forester, and Charles Fredrick Holder. Holder was a philanthropist, a passionate naturalist, author of books on marine zoology and big-game fishing, and a founder of Pasadena's Tournament of Roses and the Tuna Club of Avalon, Catalina. Pinchot became head of the Division of Forestry in the Department of Agriculture in 1898. Pinchot's influence increased enormously during the presidency of Theodore Roosevelt, and was influential in Roosevelt's decision to transfer millions of acres of forest lands to the reserves, and shared responsibility for notable advances in conservation and forestry between 1901 and 1909 with Roosevelt.

White's party had spent several days fishing, hiking, and exploring Indian mounds. The Senator thought he found a short cut back to camp but soon found himself working down the narrow runway of a deep canyon, and when at the bottom of the gorge he realized he could not go back. In trying to scale the granite canyon walls he fell and rolled fifty feet, ending with bruises. Determined, he kept going, and after several hours was about to give up hope when he saw the ocean and was able to get to a small sheltered beach. Some time later, he gained the attention of a fishing boat by waving his jacket in the air, and was rescued by the fisherman.

White was also friends and hunting companion with Theodore Roosevelt, Jr., and in July of 1910, the two men went into the Santa Ynez Mountains near Santa Barbara on a mountain lion hunt. It was said they would soon be joined by their wives, Mrs. White and Mrs. Roosevelt. Plans were being made also for a grand tour of Africa, following the trail of the elder Roosevelt. White, the article stated, was going for the purpose of getting material for a book, while the younger Roosevelt wanted to add some luster of his own to the family name and prove his prowess as a hunter. It was the intention to take a large party of sportsmen and their families on the African trip.

In May, 1927, a new type of Boy Scout was created—to be chosen from "American citizens whose achievements in outdoor activity, exploration and worthwhile adventure are of such an exceptional character as to capture the imagination of boys. . . ." Eighteen men were found worthy of the distinction which bears the title of Honorary Scout. In that list of eighteen men was Charles A. Lindbergh, Orville Wright, Kermit Roosevelt, and Stewart Edward White.

In 1932, it was written that Stewart Edward White was one of President Hoover's favorite American novelists, along with Western writer, Zane Grey, Willa Cather, Harry Leon Wilson, Thomas Nelson Page, Tarkington and Edith Wharton.

Five years later, in 1937, Stewart Edward White published a nonfiction book that was very different then his previous popular books. It was an adventure, but not the kind he had written for nearly forty years. And again, like in many of his books, he wrote from personal experience. It would be the first of several books on the subject of spirit communication.

The story of his new book began March 17, 1919. It was on that evening when a small group of friends arrived at Stewart's home with a Ouija board. A woman present that evening, which he identifies as "Betty," had little interest in the spirit game but the board repeatedly spelled out her name. She was reluctant to join the "spirit reading" again, but the board then began to spell out repeatedly, "Get a pencil." Betty had no knowledge of automatic writing, but a few days later she did get a pencil and as she sat quietly the pencil began to move across the paper without effort from her, nor did she have knowledge of what was being written. For the next few months, these "automatic writing sessions" with spirit took place. A year later, Betty was a full trance medium of a group of spirits who Stewart and Betty nicknamed *The Invisibles*. This remarkable book, *The Betty Book*, became the first of several books on the subject. The second book, *Across the Unknown* came out two years later and about the time the third book, *The Unobstructed Universe* was published in 1940, it was revealed that "Betty" was his wife, Elizabeth. Elizabeth had passed away in 1939, after twenty years of recording their experiences with the world of spirit. Although she left the physical body, Stewart continued to have contact with her from the other side, and wrote of those experiences in *The Unobstructed Universe* in which their friend "Joan" is the medium for messages and teachings from Betty.

The "Betty Books" are considered classics within the literature of spirit communication, and it was the Betty Books that brought Stewart Edward White to my attention a few years ago. It was only after reading his three spiritual books that I become curious about his other literary works, and then discovered the richness of his legacy and his impact on the history of our country.

In these nonfiction books he treated their adventure into the world of spirit in very much the same way as he did all his other adventurous journeys throughout his life. The style of writing reflected that enthusiastic adventure and exploration, even though it was a journey into the unknown, into the self, and into the after life. He was able to write about the adventures beyond the veil in very much the same passionate way he wrote about nature and the earthly frontier.

Attempting to give the reader an idea of the credibility and importance of Betty's message from the spirit group, *The Invisibles*, he explained how psychic events have to be experienced in a personal way, yet he is saying that exposure to or reading about the spiritual experiences of others can be an exciting and fulfilling experience. So if out hiking the beautiful countryside, or listening to or reading channeled wisdom, both can be an exciting journey.

In his words from his nonfiction, *Across the Unknown*, Chapter VI, Landmarks:

"In a new country a man must find his own way. The landmarks planted by his predecessors he must discover for himself. When he overtakes them, he is heartened by their evidence that others have passed this way and found the way reliable. That is the principle reason for placing landmarks, against the time when someone shall need them.

"But also there is a value in travelers' tales. They excite interest. They breathe the atmosphere of adventure in strange lands. They awaken the romance of the unexplored and the unknown, arousing us to venture.

"Before commencing the records of Betty's exploration I must emphasize one thing every writer knows. No account does more than insignificant credit to the original. And this seems to be particularly true when we deal with the far reaches of the mind. A kind of penumbra of illumination accompanies the thing itself, which is lacking in cold type. I suppose this is inevitable when we concern ourselves with a reality whose greater part is intangible, beyond the measuring ability of the brain. I cannot sufficiently stress this apparently obvious statement. Only personal experience can realize its import."

Stewart Edward White died September 18, 1946 at Hillsborough, California, where he had lived for many years. A nonfiction book completed days before his death, *With Folded Wings* was published in 1947, and another nonfiction manuscript, *The Job of Living* was published in 1948.

The legacy left to us by Stewart Edward White lives on, and nearly sixty-five years later, his works are still appreciated as they were at the opening of the twentieth century.

Linda Pendleton,
Northern California,
April, 2010

Chapter One: Spanish Days

The dominant people of California have been successively aborigines, *conquistadores*, monks, the dreamy, romantic, unenergetic peoples of Spain, the roaring mélange of Forty-nine, and finally the modern citizens, who are so distinctive that they bid fair to become a sub-subspecies of their own. This modern society has, in its evolution, something unique. To be sure, other countries also have passed through these same phases. But while the processes have consumed a leisurely five hundred years or so elsewhere, here they have been subjected to forced growth.

The tourist traveler is inclined to look upon the crumbling yet beautiful remains of the old missions, those venerable relics in a bustling modern land, as he looks upon the enduring remains of old Rome. Yet there are today many unconsidered New England farmhouses older than the oldest western mission, and there are men now living who witnessed the passing of Spanish California.

Though the existence of California had been known for centuries, and the dates of her first visitors are many hundreds of years old, nevertheless Spain attempted no actual occupation until she was forced to it by political necessity. Until that time she had little use for the country.

After early investigations had exploded her dream of more treasure cities similar to those looted by Cortés and Pizarro, her interest promptly died.

But in the latter part of the eighteenth century Spain began to awake to the importance of action. Fortunately ready to her hand was a tried and tempered weapon. Just as the modern statesmen turn to commercial penetration, so Spain turned, as always, to religious occupation. She made use of the missionary spirit and she sent forth her expeditions ostensibly for the purpose of converting the heathen. The result was the so-called *Sacred Expedition* under the leadership of Junípero Serra and Portolá. In the face of incredible hardships and discouragements, these devoted, if narrow and simple, men succeeded in establishing a string of missions from San Diego to Sonoma. The energy, self-sacrifice, and persistence of the members of this expedition furnish inspiring reading today and show clearly of what the Spanish character at its best is capable.

For the next thirty years after the founding of the first mission in 1769, the grasp of Spain on California was assured. Men who could do, suffer, and endure occupied the land. They made their mistakes in judgment and in methods, but the strong fiber of the pioneer was there.

The original *padres* were almost without exception zealous, devoted to poverty, uplifted by a fanatic desire to further their cause. The original Spanish temporal leaders were in general able, energetic, courageous, and not afraid of work or fearful of disaster.

At the end of that period, however, things began to suffer a change. The time of pioneering came to an end, and the new age of material prosperity began. Evils of various sorts crept in. The pioneer priests were in some instances replaced by men who thought more of the flesh-pot than of the altar, and whose treatment of the Indians left very much to be desired. Squabbles arose between the civil and the religious powers. Envy of the missions' immense holdings undoubtedly had its influence.

The final result of the struggle could not be avoided, and in the end the complete secularization of the missions took place, and with this inevitable change the real influence of these religious outposts came to an end.

Thus before the advent in California of the American as an American, and not as a traveler or a naturalized citizen, the mission had disappeared from the land, and the land was inhabited by a race calling itself the *gente de razón,* in presumed contradistinction to human beasts with no reasoning powers. Of this period the lay reader finds such conflicting accounts that he either is bewildered or else boldly indulges his prejudices. According to one school of writers—mainly those of modern fiction—California before the advent of the *gringo* was a sort of Arcadian paradise, populated by a people who were polite, generous, pleasure-loving, high-minded, chivalrous, aristocratic, and above all things romantic. Only with the coming of the loosely sordid, commercial, and despicable American did this Arcadia fade to the strains of dying and pathetic music. According to another school of writers—mainly authors of personal reminiscences at a time when growing antagonism was accentuating the difference in ideals—the "greaser" was a dirty, idle, shiftless, treacherous, tawdry vagabond, dwelling in a disgracefully primitive house, and backward in every aspect of civilization.

The truth, of course, lies somewhere between the two extremes, but its exact location is difficult though not impossible to determine. The influence of environment is sometimes strong, but human nature does not differ much from age to age. Racial characteristics remain approximately the same. The Californians were of several distinct classes. The upper class, which consisted of a very few families, generally included those who had held office, and whose pride led them to intermarry. Pure blood was exceedingly rare. Of even the best the majority had Indian blood; but the slightest mixture of Spanish was a sufficient claim to gentility.

Outside of these "first families," the bulk of the population came from three sources: the original military adjuncts to the missions, those brought in as settlers, and convicts imported to support one side or another in the innumerable political squabbles. These diverse elements shared one sentiment only—an aversion to work. The feeling had grown up that in order to maintain the prestige of the soldier in the eyes of the natives it was highly improper that he should ever do any labor. The settlers, of whom there were few, had themselves been induced to immigrate by rather extravagant promises of an easy life. The convicts were only what was to be expected.

If limitations of space and subject permitted, it would be pleasant to portray the romantic life of those pastoral days. Arcadian conditions were then more nearly attained than perhaps at any other time in the world's history. The picturesque, easy, idle, pleasant, fiery, aristocratic life has been elsewhere so well depicted that it has taken on the quality of rosy legend. Nobody did any more work than it pleased him to do; everybody was well-fed and happy; the women were beautiful and chaste; the men were bold, fiery, spirited, gracefully idle; life was a succession of picturesque merrymakings, lovemakings, intrigues, visits, lavish hospitalities, harmless politics, and revolutions. To be sure, there were but few signs of progressive spirit. People traveled on horseback because roads did not exist. They wore silks and diamonds, lace and satin, but their houses were crude, and conveniences were simple or entirely lacking. Their very vehicles, with wooden axles and wheels made of the cross-section of a tree, were such as an East African savage would be ashamed of. But who cared? And since no one wished improvements, why worry about them?

Certainly, judged by the standards of a truly progressive race, the Spanish occupation had many shortcomings. Agriculture was so little known that at times the country nearly starved. Contemporary travelers mention this fact with wonder. "There is," says Ryan, "very little land under cultivation in the vicinity of Monterey. That which strikes the foreigner most is the utter neglect in which the soil is left and the indifference with which the most charming sites are regarded. In the hands of the English and Americans, Monterey would be a beautiful town adorned with gardens and orchards and surrounded with picturesque walks and drives. The natives are, unfortunately, too ignorant to appreciate and too indolent even to attempt such improvement." And Captain Charles Wilkes asserts that "notwithstanding the immense number of domestic animals in the country, the Californians were too lazy to make butter or cheese, and even milk was rare. If there was a little good soap and leather occasionally found, the people were too indolent to make them in any quantity. The earth was simply scratched a few inches by a mean and ill-contrived plow. When the ground had been turned up by repeated scratching, it was hoed down and the clods broken by dragging over it huge branches of trees. Threshing was performed by spreading the cut grain on a spot of hard ground, treading it with cattle, and after taking off the straw throwing the remainder up in the breeze, much was lost and what was saved was foul."

General shiftlessness and inertia extended also to those branches wherein the Californian was supposed to excel. Even in the matter of cattle and sheep, the stock was very inferior to that brought into the country by the Americans, and such a thing as crossing stock or improving the breed of either cattle or horses was never thought of. The cattle were long-horned, rough-skinned animals, and the beef was tough and coarse. The sheep, while of Spanish stock, were very far from being Spanish merino. Their wool was of the poorest quality, entirely unfit for exportation, and their meat was not a favorite food.

There were practically no manufactures on the whole coast. The inhabitants depended for all luxuries and necessities on foreign trade, and in exchange gave hide and tallow from the semi-wild cattle that roamed the hills. Even this trade was discouraged by heavy import duties which amounted at times to one hundred per cent of the value. Such conditions naturally led to extensive smuggling which was connived at by most officials, high and low, and even by the monks of the missions themselves.

Although the chief reason for Spanish occupancy was to hold the country, the provisions for defense were not only inadequate but careless. Thomes says, in *Land and Sea*, that the fort at Monterey was "armed with four long brass nine-pounders, the handsomest guns that I ever saw all covered with scroll work and figures. They were mounted on ruined and decayed carriages. Two of them were pointed toward the planet Venus, and the other two were depressed so that had they been loaded or fired the balls would have startled the people on the other side of the hemisphere." This condition was typical of those throughout the so-called armed forts of California.

The picture thus presented is unjustly shaded, of course, for Spanish California had its ideal, noble, and romantic side. In a final estimate no one could say where the balance would be struck; but our purpose is not to strike a final balance. We are here endeavoring to analyze the reasons why the task of the American conquerors was so easy, and to explain the facility with which the original population was thrust aside.

It is a sometimes rather annoying anomaly of human nature that the races and individuals about whom are woven the most indestructible mantles of romance are generally those who, from the standpoint of economic stability or solid moral quality, are the most variable. We staid and sober citizens are inclined to throw an aura of picturesqueness about such creatures as the Stuarts, the dissipated Virginian cavaliers, the happy-go-lucky barren artists of the Latin Quarter, the fiery touchiness of that so-called chivalry which was one of the least important features of Southern life, and so on. We staid and sober citizens generally object strenuously to living in actual contact with the unpunctuality, unreliability, unreasonableness, shiftlessness, and general irresponsibility that are the invariable concomitants of this picturesqueness. At a safe distance we prove less critical. We even go so far as to regard this unfamiliar life as a mental anodyne or antidote to the rigid responsibility of our own everyday existence. We use these historical accounts for moral relaxation, much as some financiers or statisticians are said to read cheap detective stories for complete mental relaxation.

But, the Californian's undoubtedly admirable qualities of generosity, kindheartedness (whenever narrow prejudice or very lofty pride was not touched), hospitality, and all the rest, proved, in the eyes of a practical people confronted with a large and practical job, of little value in view of his predominantly negative qualities. A man with all the time in the world rarely gets on with a man who has no time at all. The newcomer had his house to put in order; and it was a very big house.

The American wanted to get things done at once; the Californian could see no especial reason for doing them at all. Even when his short-lived enthusiasm happened to be aroused, it was for action tomorrow rather than today.

For all his amiable qualities, the mainspring of the Californian's conduct was at bottom the impression he could make upon others. The magnificence of his apparel and his accoutrement indicated no feeling for luxury but rather a fondness for display. His pride and quick-tempered honor were rooted in a desire to stand well in the eyes of his equals, not in a desire to stand well with himself. In consequence he had not the builder's fundamental instinct. He made no effort to supply himself with anything that did not satisfy this amiable desire. The contradictions of his conduct, therefore, become comprehensible. We begin to see why he wore silks and satins and why he neglected what to us are necessities. We see why he could display such admirable carriage in rough-riding and lassoing grizzlies, and yet seemed to possess such feeble military efficiency. We comprehend his generous hospitality coupled with his often narrow and suspicious cruelty. In fact, all the contrasts of his character and action begin to be clear. His displacement was natural when confronted by a people who, whatever their serious faults, had wants and desires that came from within, who possessed the instinct to create and to hold the things that would gratify those desires, and who, in the final analysis, began to care for other men's opinions only after they had satisfied their own needs and desires.

Chapter Two: The American Occupation

From the earliest period Spain had discouraged foreign immigration into California. Her object was neither to attract settlers nor to develop the country, but to retain political control of it, and to make of it a possible asylum for her own people. Fifty years after the founding of the first mission at San Diego, California had only thirteen inhabitants of foreign birth. Most of these had become naturalized citizens, and so were in name Spanish. Of these but three were American!

Subsequent to 1822, however, the number of foreign residents rapidly increased. These people were mainly of substantial character, possessing a real interest in the country and an intention of permanent settlement.

Most of them became naturalized, married Spanish women, acquired property, and became trusted citizens. In marked contrast to their neighbors, they invariably displayed the greatest energy and enterprise. They were generally liked by the natives, and such men as Hartnell, Richardson, David Spence, Nicholas Den, and many others, lived lives and left reputations to be envied.

Between 1830 and 1840, however, Americans of a different type began to present themselves. Southwest of the Missouri River the ancient town of Santa Fe attracted trappers and traders of all nations and from all parts of the great West. There they met to exchange their wares and to organize new expeditions into the remote territories. Some of them naturally found their way across the western mountains into California.

One of the most notable was James Pattie, whose personal narrative is well worth reading. These men were bold, hardy, rough, energetic, with little patience for the refinements of life—in fact, diametrically opposed in character to the easy-going inhabitants of California.

Contempt on the one side and distrust on the other were inevitable. The trappers and traders, together with the deserters from whalers and other ships, banded together in small communities of the rough type familiar to any observer of our frontier communities. They looked down upon and despised the "greasers," who in turn did everything in their power to harass them by political and other means.

At first isolated parties, such as those of Jedediah Smith, the Patties, and some others, had been imprisoned or banished eastward over the Rockies. The pressure of increasing numbers, combined with the rather idle carelessness into which all California-Spanish regulations seemed at length to fall, later nullified this drastic policy.

Notorious among these men was one Isaac Graham, an American trapper, who had become weary of wandering and had settled near Natividad. There he established a small distillery, and in consequence drew about him all the rough and idle characters of the country. Some were trappers, some sailors; a few were Mexicans and renegade Indians. Over all of these Graham obtained an absolute control. They were most of them of a belligerent nature and expert shots, accustomed to taking care of themselves in the wilds. This little band, though it consisted of only thirty-nine members, was therefore considered formidable.

A rumor that these people were plotting an uprising for the purpose of overturning the government aroused Governor Alvarado to action. It is probable that the rumors in question were merely the reports of boastful drunken vaporings and would better have been ignored. However, at this time Alvarado, recently arisen to power through the usual revolutionary tactics, felt himself not entirely secure in his new position. He needed some distraction, and he therefore seized upon the rumor of Graham's uprising as a means of solidifying his influence—an expedient not unknown to modern rulers. He therefore ordered the prefect Castro to arrest the party. This was done by surprise. Graham and his companions were taken from their beds, placed upon a ship at Monterey, and exiled to San Blas, to be eventually delivered to the Mexican authorities. There they were held in prison for some months, but being at last released through the efforts of an American lawyer, most of them returned to California rather better off than before their arrest. It is typical of the vacillating Californian policy of the day that, on their return, Graham and his riflemen were at once made use of by one of the revolutionary parties as a reinforcement to their military power!

By 1840 the foreign population had by these rather desultory methods been increased to a few over four hundred souls. The majority could not be described as welcome guests. They had rarely come into the country with the deliberate intention of settling but rather as a traveler's chance.

In November, 1841, however, two parties of quite a different character arrived. They were the first true immigrants into California, and their advent is significant as marking the beginning of the end of the old order. One of these parties entered by the Salt Lake Trail, and was the forerunner of the many pioneers over that great central route.

The other came by Santa Fe, over the trail that had by now become so well marked that they hardly suffered even inconvenience on their journey. The first party arrived at Monte Diablo in the north, the other at San Gabriel Mission in the south. Many brought their families with them, and they came with the evident intention of settling in California.

The arrival of these two parties presented to the Mexican Government a problem that required immediate solution. Already in anticipation of such an event it had been provided that nobody who had not obtained a legal passport should be permitted to remain in the country; and that even old settlers, unless naturalized, should be required to depart unless they procured official permission to remain. Naturally none of the new arrivals had received notice of this law, and they were in consequence unprovided with the proper passports. Legally they should have been forced at once to turn about and return by the way they came.

Actually it would have been inhuman, if not impossible, to have forced them at that season of the year to attempt the mountains. General Vallejo, always broad-minded in his policies, used discretion in the matter and provided those in his district with temporary permits to remain. He required only a bond signed by other Americans who had been longer in the country.

Alvarado and Vallejo at once notified the Mexican Government of the arrival of these strangers, and both expressed fear that other and larger parties would follow. These fears were very soon realized.

Succeeding expeditions settled in the State with the evident intention of remaining. No serious effort was made by the California authorities to keep them out. From time to time, to be sure, formal objection was raised and regulations were passed. However, as a matter of plain practicability, it was manifestly impossible to prevent parties from starting across the plains, or to inform the people living in the Eastern States of the regulations adopted by California. It must be remembered that communication at that time was extraordinarily slow and broken. It would have been cruel and unwarranted to drive away those who had already arrived. And even were such a course to be contemplated, a garrison would have been necessary at every mountain pass on the East and North, and at every crossing of the Colorado River, as well as at every port along the coast. The government in California had not men sufficient to handle its own few antique guns in its few coastwise forts, let alone a surplus for the purpose just described. And to cap all, provided the garrisons had been available and could have been placed, it would have been physically impossible to have supplied them with provisions for even a single month.

Truth to tell, the newcomers of this last class were not personally objectionable to the Californians. The Spanish considered them no different from those of their own blood. Had it not been for an uneasiness lest the enterprise of the American settlers should in time overcome Californian interests, had it not been for repeated orders from Mexico itself, and had it not been for reports that ten thousand Mormons had recently left Illinois for California, it is doubtful if much attention would have been paid to the first immigrants.

Westward migration at this time was given an added impetus by the Oregon question. The status of Oregon had long been in doubt. Both England and the United States were inclined to claim priority of occupation. The boundary between Canada and the United States had not yet been decided upon between the two countries. Though they had agreed upon the compromise of joint occupation of the disputed land, this arrangement did not meet with public approval. The land-hungry took a particular interest in the question and joined their voices with those of men actuated by more patriotic motives. In public meetings which were held throughout the country this joint occupation convention was explained and discussed, and its abrogation was demanded. These meetings helped to form the patriotic desire.

Senator Tappan once said that thirty thousand settlers with their thirty thousand rifles in the valley of the Columbia would quickly settle all questions of title to the country. This saying was adopted as the slogan for a campaign in the West. It had the same inspiring effect as the later famous "54-40 or fight." People were aroused as in the olden times they had been aroused to the crusades. It became a form of mental contagion to talk of, and finally to accomplish, the journey to the Northwest. Though no accurate records were kept, it is estimated that in 1843 over 800 people crossed to Willamette Valley. By 1845 this immigration had increased to fully 3000 within the year.

Because of these conditions the Oregon Trail had become a national highway. Starting at Independence, which is a suburb of the present Kansas City, it set out over the rolling prairie. At that time the wide plains were bright with wild flowers and teeming with game. Elk, antelope, wild turkeys, buffalo, deer, and a great variety of smaller creatures supplied sport and food in plenty. Wood and water were in every ravine; the abundant grass was sufficient to maintain the swarming hordes of wild animals and to give rich pasture to horses and oxen. The journey across these prairies, while long and hard, could rarely have been tedious. Tremendous thunderstorms succeeded the sultry heat of the West, an occasional cyclone added excitement; the cattle were apt to stampede senselessly; and, while the Indian had not yet developed the hostility that later made a journey across the plains so dangerous, nevertheless the possibilities of theft were always near enough at hand to keep the traveler alert and interested. Then there was the sandy country of the Platte River with its buffalo--buffalo by the hundreds of thousands, as far as the eye could reach—a marvelous sight: and beyond that again the Rockies, by way of Fort Laramie and South Pass.

Beyond Fort Hall, the Oregon Trail and the trail for California divided.

And at this point there began the terrible part of the journey—the arid, alkaline, thirsty desert, short of game, horrible in its monotony, deadly with its thirst. It is no wonder that, weakened by their sufferings in this inferno, so many of the immigrants looked upon the towering walls of the Sierras with a sinking of the heart.

While at first most of the influx of settlers was by way of Oregon, later the stories of the new country that made their way eastward induced travelers to go direct to California itself. The immigration, both from Oregon in the North and by the route over the Sierras, increased so rapidly that in 1845 there were probably about 700 Americans in the district. Those coming over the Sierras by the Carson Sink and Salt Lake trails arrived first of all at the fort built by Captain Sutter at the junction of the American and Sacramento rivers.

Captain Sutter was a man of Swiss parentage who had arrived in San Francisco in 1839 without much capital and with only the assets of considerable ability and great driving force. From the Governor he obtained grant of a large tract of land "somewhere in the interior" for the purposes of colonization. His colonists consisted of one German, four other white men, and eight Kanakas.

The then Governor, Alvarado, thought this rather a small beginning, but advised him to take out naturalization papers and to select a location. Sutter set out on his somewhat vague quest with a four-oared boat and two small schooners, loaded with provisions, implements, ammunition, and three small cannon.

Besides his original party he took an Indian boy and a dog, the latter proving by no means the least useful member of the company. He found at the junction of the American and Sacramento rivers the location that appealed to him, and there he established himself. His knack with the Indians soon enlisted their services. He seems to have been able to keep his agreements with them and at the same time to maintain rigid discipline and control.

Within an incredibly short time he had established a feudal barony at his fort. He owned eleven square leagues of land, four thousand two hundred cattle, two thousand horses, and about as many sheep. His trade in beaver skins was most profitable. He maintained a force of trappers who were always welcome at his fort, and whom he generously kept without cost to themselves. He taught the Indians blanket-weaving, hat-making, and other trades, and he even organized them into military companies.

The fort which he built was enclosed on four sides and of imposing dimensions and convenience. It mounted twelve pieces of artillery, supported a regular garrison of forty in uniform, and contained within its walls a blacksmith shop, a distillery, a flour mill, a cannery, and space for other necessary industries. Outside the walls of the fort Captain Sutter raised wheat, oats, and barley in quantity, and even established an excellent fruit and vegetable garden.

Indeed, in every way Captain Sutter's environment and the results of his enterprises were in significant contrast to the inactivity and backwardness of his neighbors. He showed what an energetic man could accomplish with exactly the same human powers and material tools as had always been available to the Californians. Sutter himself was a rather short, thick-set man, exquisitely neat, of military bearing, carrying himself with what is called the true old-fashioned courtesy. He was a man of great generosity and of high spirit. His defect was an excess of ambition which in the end o'erleaped itself. There is no doubt that his first expectation was to found an independent state within the borders of California. His loyalty to the Americans was, however, never questioned, and the fact that his lands were gradually taken from him, and that he died finally in comparative poverty, is a striking comment on human injustice.

The important point for us at present is that Sutter's Fort happened to be exactly on the line of the overland immigration. For the trail-weary traveler it was the first stopping-place after crossing the high Sierras to the promised land. Sutter's natural generosity of character induced him always to treat these men with the greatest kindness. He made his profits from such as wished to get rid of their oxen and wagons in exchange for the commodities which he had to offer. But there is no doubt that the worthy captain displayed the utmost liberality in dealing with those whom poverty had overtaken. On several occasions he sent out expeditions at his personal cost to rescue parties caught in the mountains by early snows or other misfortunes along the road. Especially did he go to great expense in the matter of the ill-fated Donner party, who, it will be remembered, spent the winter near Truckee, and were reduced to cannibalism to avoid starvation. [See *The Passing of the Frontier*, in "The Chronicles of America."]

Now Sutter had, of course, been naturalized in order to obtain his grant of land. He had also been appointed an official of the California-Mexican Government. Taking advantage of this fact, he was accustomed to issue permits or passports to the immigrants, permitting them to remain in the country. This gave the immigrants a certain limited standing, but, as they were not Mexican citizens, they were disqualified from holding land. Nevertheless Sutter used his good offices in showing desirable locations to the would-be settlers. (It is to be remarked that, prior to the gold rush, American settlements did not take place in the Spanish South but in the unoccupied North. In 1845 Castro and Castillero made a tour through the Sacramento Valley and the northern regions to inquire about the new arrivals.

Castro displayed no personal uneasiness at their presence and made no attempt or threat to deport them.)

As far as the Californians were concerned, there was little rivalry or interference between the immigrants and the natives. Their interests did not as yet conflict. Nevertheless the central Mexican Government continued its commands to prevent any and all immigration. It was rather well justified by its experience in Texas, where settlement had ended by final absorption. The local Californian authorities were thus thrust between the devil and the deep blue sea. They were constrained by the very positive and repeated orders from their home government to keep out all immigration and to eject those already on the ground. On the other hand, the means for doing so were entirely lacking, and the present situation did not seem to them alarming.

Thus matters drifted along until the Mexican War. For a considerable time before actual hostilities broke out, it was well known throughout the country that they were imminent. Every naval and military commander was perfectly aware that, sooner or later, war was inevitable. Many had received their instructions in case of that eventuality, and most of the others had individual plans to be put into execution at the earliest possible moment. Indeed, as early as 1842 Commodore Jones, being misinformed of a state of war, raced with what he supposed to be English war-vessels from South America, entered the port of Monterey hastily, captured the fort, and raised the American flag. The next day he discovered that not only was there no state of war, but that he had not even raced British ships! The flag was thereupon hauled down, the Mexican emblem substituted, appropriate apologies and salutes were rendered, and the incident was considered closed. The easy-going Californians accepted the apology promptly and cherished no rancor for the mistake.

In the meantime Thomas O. Larkin, a very substantial citizen of long standing in the country, had been appointed consul, and in addition received a sum of six dollars a day to act as secret agent. It was hoped that his great influence would avail to inspire the Californians with a desire for peaceful annexation to the United States. In case that policy failed, he was to use all means to separate them from Mexico, and so isolate them from their natural alliances. He was furthermore to persuade them that England, France, and Russia had sinister designs on their liberty. It was hoped that his good offices would slowly influence public opinion, and that, on the declaration of open war with Mexico, the United States flag could be hoisted in California not only without opposition but with the consent and approval of the inhabitants. This type of peaceful conquest had a very good chance of success. Larkin possessed the confidence of the better class of Californians and he did his duty faithfully.

Just at this moment a picturesque, gallant, ambitious, dashing, and rather unscrupulous character appeared inopportunely on the horizon. His name was John C. Frémont. He was the son of a French father and a Virginia mother. He was thirty-two years old, and was married to the daughter of Thomas H. Benton, United States Senator from Missouri and a man of great influence in the country. Possessed of an adventurous spirit, considerable initiative, and great persistence, Frémont had already performed the feat of crossing the Sierra Nevadas by way of Carson River and Johnson Pass, and had also explored the Columbia River and various parts of the Northwest. Frémont now entered California by way of Walker Lake and the Truckee, and reached Sutter's Fort in 1845. He then turned southward to meet a division of his party under Joseph Walker.

His expedition was friendly in character, with the object of surveying a route westward to the Pacific, and then northward to Oregon. It supposedly possessed no military importance whatever. But his turning south to meet Walker instead of north, where ostensibly his duty called him, immediately aroused the suspicions of the Californians. Though ordered to leave the district, he refused compliance, and retired to a place called Gavilán Peak, where he erected fortifications and raised the United States flag. Probably Frémont's intentions were perfectly friendly and peaceful. He made, however, a serious blunder in withdrawing within fortifications. After various threats by the Californians but no performance in the way of attack, he withdrew and proceeded by slow marches to Sutter's Fort and thence towards the north.

Near Klamath Lake he was overtaken by Lieutenant Gillespie, who delivered to him certain letters and papers. Frémont thereupon calmly turned south with the pick of his men.

In the meantime the Spanish sub-prefect, Guerrero, had sent word to Larkin that a multitude of foreigners, having come into California and bought property, a right of naturalized foreigners only, and that he was under necessity of notifying the authorities in each town to inform such purchasers that the transactions were invalid, and that "they themselves were subject to be expelled." This action at once caused widespread consternation among the settlers. They remembered the deportation of Graham and his party some years before, and were both alarmed and thoroughly convinced that defensive measures were necessary.

Frémont's return at precisely this moment seemed to them very significant. He was a United States army officer at the head of a government expedition.

When on his way to the North he had been overtaken by Gillespie, an officer of the United States Navy. Gillespie had delivered to him certain papers, whereupon he had immediately returned. There seemed no other interpretation of these facts than that the Government at Washington was prepared to uphold by force the American settlers in California.

This reasoning, logical as it seems, proves mistaken in the perspective of the years. Gillespie, it is true, delivered some letters to Frémont, but it is extremely unlikely they contained instructions having to do with interference in Californian affairs. Gillespie, at the same time that he brought these dispatches to Frémont, brought also instructions to Larkin creating the confidential agency above described, and these instructions specifically forbade interference with Californian affairs.

It is unreasonable to suppose that contradictory dispatches were sent to one or another of these two men. Many years later Frémont admitted that the dispatch to Larkin was what had been communicated to him by Gillespie. His words are: "This officer [Gillespie] informed me also that he was directed by the Secretary of State to acquaint me with his instructions to the consular agent, Mr. Larkin." Reading Frémont's character, understanding his ambitions, interpreting his later lawless actions that resulted in his court-martial, realizing the recklessness of his spirit, and his instinct to take chances, one comes to the conclusion that it is more than likely that his move was a gamble on probabilities rather than a result of direct orders.

Be this as it may, the mere fact of Frémont's turning south decided the alarmed settlers, and led to the so-called "Bear Flag Revolution." A number of settlers decided that it would be expedient to capture Sonoma, where under Vallejo were nine cannon and some two hundred muskets. It was, in fact, a sort of military station. The capture proved to be a very simple matter. Thirty-two or thirty-three men appeared at dawn, before Vallejo's house, under Merritt and Semple. They entered the house suddenly, called upon

Jacob Leese, Vallejo's son-in-law, to interpret, and demanded immediate surrender.

Richman says "Leese was surprised at the 'rough looks' of the Americans. Semple he describes as 'six feet six inches tall, and about fifteen inches in diameter, dressed in greasy buckskin from neck to foot, and with a fox-skin cap.'"

The prisoners were at once sent by these raiders to Frémont, who was at that time on the American River. He immediately disclaimed any part in the affair. However, instead of remaining entirely aloof, he gave further orders that Leese, who was still in attendance as interpreter, should be arrested, and also that the prisoners should be confined in Sutter's Fort. He thus definitely and officially entered the movement. Soon thereafter Frémont started south through Sonoma, collecting men as he went.

The following quotation from a contemporary writer is interesting and illuminating. "A vast cloud of dust appeared at first, and thence in long files emerged this wildest of wild parties. Frémont rode ahead, a spare active looking man, with such an eye! He was dressed in a blouse and leggings, and wore a felt hat. After him came five Delaware Indians who were his bodyguard. They had charge of two baggage-horses. The rest, many of them blacker than Indians, rode two and two, the rifle held by one hand across the pummel of the saddle. The dress of these men was principally a long loose coat of deerskin tied with thongs in front, trousers of the same. The saddles were of various fashions, though these and a large drove of horses and a brass field gun were things they had picked up in California."

Meantime, the Americans who had collected in Sonoma, under the lead of William B. Ide, raised the flag of revolution—"a standard of somewhat uncertain origin as regards the cotton cloth whereof it was made," writes Royce. On this, they painted with berry juice "something that they called a Bear." By this capture of Sonoma, and its subsequent endorsement by Frémont, Larkin's instructions that is, to secure California by quiet diplomatic means—were absolutely nullified. A second result was that Englishmen in California were much encouraged to hope for English intervention and protection. The Vallejo circle had always been strongly favorable to the United States. The effect of this raid and capture by United States citizens, with a United States officer endorsing the action, may well be guessed.

Inquiries and protests were lodged by the California authorities with Sloat and Lieutenant Montgomery of the United States naval forces. Just what effect these protests would have had, and just the temperature of the hot water in which the dashing Frémont would have found himself, is a matter of surmise. He had gambled strongly—on his own responsibility or at least at the unofficial suggestion of Benton—on an early declaration of war with Mexico. Failing such a declaration, he would be in a precarious diplomatic position, and must by mere force of automatic Discipline have been heavily punished. However the dice fell for him.

War with Mexico was almost immediately an actual fact. Frémont's injection into the revolution had been timed at the happiest possible moment for him.

The *Bear Flag Revolution* took place on June 14,1846. On July 7 the American flag was hoisted over the post at Monterey by Commodore Sloat. Though he had knowledge from June 5 of a state of war, this knowledge, apparently, he had shared neither with his officers nor with the public, and he exhibited a want of initiative and vigor which is in striking contrast to Frémont's ambition and overzeal.

Shortly after this incident Commodore Sloat was allowed to return "by reason of ill health," as has been heretofore published in most histories. His undoubted recall gave room to Commodore Robert Stockton, to whom Sloat not only turned over the command of the naval forces, but whom he also directed to "assume command of the forces and operations on shore."

Stockton at once invited Frémont to enlist under his command, and the invitation was accepted. The entire forces moved south by sea and land for the purpose of subduing southern California. This end was temporarily accomplished with almost ridiculous ease. At this distance of time, allowing all obvious explanations of lack of training, meager equipment, and internal dissension, we find it a little difficult to understand why the Californians did not make a better stand. Most of the so-called battles were a sort of *opera bouffe*. Californians entrenched with cannon were driven contemptuously forth, without casualties, by a very few men. For example, a lieutenant and nine men were sufficient to hold Santa Barbara in subjection. Indeed, the conquest was too easy, for, lulled into false security, Stockton departed, leaving as he supposed sufficient men to hold the country. The Californians managed to get some coherence into their councils, attacked the Americans, and drove them forth from their garrisons.

Stockton and Frémont immediately started south. In the meantime an overland party under General Kearny had been dispatched from the East. His instructions were rather broad. He was to take in such small sections of the country as New Mexico and Arizona, leaving sufficient garrisons on his way to California. As a result, though his command at first numbered 1657 men, he arrived in the latter state with only about 100. From Warner's Ranch in the mountains he sent word to Stockton that he had arrived. Gillespie, whom the Commodore at once dispatched with thirty-nine men to meet and conduct him to San Diego, joined Kearny near San Luis Rey Mission.

A force of Californians, however, under command of one Andrés Pico had been hovering about the hills watching the Americans. It was decided to attack this force. Twenty men were detailed under Captain Johnston for the purpose. At dawn on the morning of the 6th of December the

Americans charged upon the Californian camp. The Californians promptly decamped after having delivered a volley which resulted in killing Johnston. The Americans at once pursued them hotly, became much scattered, and were
turned upon by the fleeing enemy. The Americans were poorly mounted after their journey, their weapons were now empty, and they were unable to give mutual aid. The Spanish were armed with lances, pistols, and the deadly *riata*. Before the rearguard could come up, sixteen of the total American force were killed and nineteen badly wounded. This battle of San Pascual, as it was called, is interesting as being the only engagement in which the Californians got the upper hand. Whether their Parthian tactics were the result of a preconceived policy or were merely an expedient of the moment, it is impossible to say. The battle is also notable because the well-known scout, Kit Carson, took part in it.

The forces of Stockton and Kearny joined a few days later, and very soon a conflict of authority arose between the leaders. It was a childish affair throughout, and probably at bottom arose from Frémont's usual over-ambitious designs. To Kearny had undoubtedly been given, by the properly constituted authorities, the command of all the land operations. Stockton, however, claimed to hold supreme land command by instructions from Commodore Sloat already quoted. Through the internal evidence of Stockton's letters and proclamations, it seems he was a trifle inclined to be bombastic and high-flown, to usurp authority, and perhaps to consider himself and his operations of more importance than they actually were. However, he was an officer disciplined and trained to obedience, and his absurd contention is not in character. It may be significant that he had promised to appoint Frémont Governor of California, a promise that naturally could not be fulfilled if Kearny's authority were fully recognized.

Furthermore, at this moment Frémont was at the zenith of his career, and his influence in such matters was considerable. As Hittell says, "At this time and for some time afterwards, Frémont was represented as a sort of young lion. The several trips he had made across the continent, and the several able and interesting reports he had published over his name attracted great public attention. He was hardly ever mentioned except in a high-flown hyperbolical phrase. Benton was one of the most influential men of his day, and it soon became well understood that the surest way of reaching the father-in-law's favor was by furthering the son-in-law's prospects; everybody that wished to court Benton praised Frémont. Besides this political influence Benton exerted in Frémont's behalf, there was an almost equally strong social influence." It might be added that the nature of his public service had been such as to throw him on his own responsibility, and that he had always gambled with fortune, as in the Bear Flag Revolution already mentioned. His star had ever been in the ascendant. He was a spoiled child of fortune at this time, and bitterly and haughtily resented any check to his ambition. The mixture of his blood gave him that fine sense of the dramatic which so easily descends to posing. His actual accomplishment was without doubt great; but his own appreciation of that accomplishment was also undoubtedly great. He was one of those interesting characters whose activities are so near the line between great deeds and charlatanism that it is sometimes difficult to segregate the pose from the performance.

The end of this row for precedence did not come until after the so-called battles at the San Gabriel River and on the Mesa on January 8 and 9, 1847. The first of these conflicts is so typical that it is worth a paragraph of description.

The Californians were posted on the opposite bank of the river. They had about five hundred men, and two pieces of artillery well placed. The bank was elevated some forty feet above the stream and possibly four or six hundred back from the water. The American forces, all told, consisted of about five hundred men, but most of them were dismounted. The tactics were exceedingly simple. The Americans merely forded the river, dragged their guns across, put them in position, and calmly commenced a vigorous bombardment. After about an hour and a half of circling about and futile half-attacks, the Californians withdrew. The total American loss in this and the succeeding "battle," called that of the Mesa, was three killed and twelve wounded.

After this latter battle, the Californians broke completely and hurtled toward the North. Beyond Los Angeles, near San Fernando, they ran head-on into Frémont and his California battalion marching overland from the North. Frémont had just learned of Stockton's defeat of the Californians and, as usual, he seized the happy chance the gods had offered him. He made haste to assure the Californians through a messenger that they would do well to negotiate with him rather than with Stockton. To these suggestions the Californians yielded. Commissioners appointed by both sides then met at Cahuenga on January 13, and elaborated a treaty by which the Californians agreed to surrender their arms and not to serve again during the war, whereupon the victors allowed them to leave the country. Frémont at once proceeded to Los Angeles, where he reported to Kearny and Stockton what had happened.

In accordance with his foolish determination, Stockton still refused to acknowledge Kearny's direct authority. He appointed Frémont Governor of California, which was one mistake; and Frémont accepted, which was another. Undoubtedly the latter thought that his pretensions would be supported by personal influence in Washington. From former experience he had every reason to believe so. In this case, however, he reckoned beyond the resources of even his powerful father-in-law. Kearny, who seems to have been a direct old war-dog, resolved at once to test his authority. He ordered Frémont to muster the California battalion into the regular service, under his (Kearny's) command; or, if the men did not wish to do this, to discharge them. This order did not in the least please Frémont. He attempted to open negotiations, but Kearny was in no manner disposed to talk. He said curtly that he had given his orders, and merely wished to know whether or not they would be obeyed. To this, and from one army officer to another, there could be but one answer, and that was in the affirmative.

Colonel Mason opportunely arrived from Washington with instructions to Frémont either to join his regiment or to resume the explorations on which he had originally been sent to this country. Frémont was still pretending to be Governor, but with nothing to govern. His game was losing at Washington. He could not know this, however, and for some time continued to persist in his absurd claims to governorship. Finally he begged permission of Kearny to form an expedition against Mexico. But it was rather late in the day for the spoiled child to ask for favors, and the permission was refused. Upon his return to Washington under further orders, Frémont was court-martialed, and was found guilty of mutiny, disobedience, and misconduct. He was ordered dismissed from the service, but was pardoned by President Polk in view of his past services. He refused this pardon and resigned.

Frémont was a picturesque figure with a great deal of personal magnetism and dash. The halo of romance has been fitted to his head. There is no doubt that he was a good wilderness traveler, a keen lover of adventure, and a likable personality. He was, however, over-ambitious; he advertised himself altogether too well; and he presumed on the undoubtedly great personal influence he possessed. He has been nicknamed the Pathfinder, but a better title would be the Pathfollower. He found no paths that had not already been traversed by men before him. Unless the silly sentiment that persistently glorifies such despicable characters as the English Stuarts continues to surround this interesting character with fallacious romance, Frémont will undoubtedly take his place in history below men now more obscure but more solid than he was. His services and his ability were both great. If he, his friends, and historians had been content to rest his fame on actualities, his position would be high and honorable. The presumption of so much more than the man actually did or was has the unfortunate effect of minimizing his real accomplishment.

Chapter Three: Law—Military and Civil

The military conquest of California was now an accomplished fact. As long as hostilities should continue in Mexico, California must remain under a military government, and such control was at once inaugurated.

The questions to be dealt with, as may well be imagined, were delicate in the extreme. In general the military Governors handled such questions with tact and efficiency. This ability was especially true in the case of Colonel Mason, who succeeded General Kearny. The understanding displayed by this man in holding back the over-eager Americans on one side, and in mollifying the sensitive Californians on the other, is worthy of all admiration.

The Mexican laws were, in lack of any others, supposed to be enforced. Under this system all trials, except of course those having to do with military affairs, took place before officials called *alcades,* who acknowledged no higher authority than the Governor himself, and enforced the laws as autocrats. The new military Governors took over the old system bodily and appointed new *alcaldes* where it seemed necessary.

The new *alcaldes* neither knew nor cared anything about the old Mexican law and its provisions. This disregard cannot be wondered at, for even a cursory examination of the legal forms convinces one that they were meant more for the enormous leisure of the old times than for the necessities of the new. In the place of Mexican law each *alcalde* attempted to substitute his own sense of justice and what recollection of common-law principles he might be able to summon. These common-law principles were not technical in the modern sense of the word, nor were there any printed or written statutes containing them. In this case they were simply what could be recalled by non-technical men of the way in which business had been conducted and disputes had been arranged back in their old homes. But their main reliance was on their individual sense of justice. As Hittell points out, even well-read lawyers who happened to be made *alcaldes* soon came to pay little attention to technicalities and to seek the merit of cases without regard to rules or forms. All the administration of the law was in the hands of these *alcaldes*. Mason, who once made the experiment of appointing a special court at Sutter's Fort to try a man known as Growling Smith for the murder of Indians, afterwards declared that he would not do it again except in the most extraordinary emergency, as the precedent was bad.

As may well be imagined, this uniquely individualistic view of the law made interesting legal history. Many of the incumbents were of the rough diamond type. Stories innumerable are related of them. They had little regard for the external dignity of the court, but they strongly insisted on its discipline. Many of them sat with their feet on the desk, chewing tobacco, and whittling a stick. During a trial one of the counsel referred to his opponent as an "oscillating Tarquín." The judge roared out "A what?"

"An oscillating Tarquín, your honor."

The judge's chair came down with a thump. "If this honorable court knows herself, and she thinks she do, that remark is an insult to this honorable court, and you are fined two ounces."

Expostulation was cut short.

"Silence, sir! This honorable court won't tolerate cussings and she never goes back on her decisions!"

And she didn't!

Nevertheless a sort of rough justice was generally accomplished. These men felt a responsibility. In addition they possessed a grim commonsense earned by actual experience.

There is an instance of a priest from Santa Clara, sued before the *alcalde* of San José for a breach of contract. His plea was that as a churchman he was not amenable to civil law. The American decided that, while he could not tell what peculiar privileges a clergyman enjoyed as a priest, it was quite evident that when he departed from his religious calling and entered into a secular bargain with a citizen he placed himself on the same footing as the citizen, and should be required like anybody else to comply with his agreement. This principle, which was good sense, has since become good law.

The *alcalde* refused to be bound by trivial concerns. A Mexican was accused of stealing a pair of leggings. He was convicted and fined three ounces for stealing, while the prosecuting witness was also fined one ounce for bothering the court with such a complaint. On another occasion the defendant, on being fined, was found to be totally insolvent. The *alcalde* thereupon ordered the plaintiff to pay the fine and costs for the reason that the court could not be expected to sit without remuneration. Though this naive system worked out well enough in the new and primitive community, nevertheless thinking men realized that it could be for a short time only.

As long as the war with Mexico continued, naturally California was under military Governors, but on the declaration of peace military government automatically ceased. Unfortunately, owing to strong controversies as to slavery or non-slavery, Congress passed no law organizing California as a territory; and the status of the newly-acquired possession was far from clear. The people held that, in the absence of congressional action, they had the right to provide for their own government. On the other hand, General Riley contended that the laws of California obtained until supplanted by act of Congress. He was under instructions as Governor to enforce this view, which was, indeed, sustained by judicial precedents. But for precedents the inhabitants cared little. They resolved to call a constitutional convention. After considerable negotiation and thought, Governor Riley resolved to accede to the wishes of the people. An election of delegates was called and the constitutional convention met at Monterey, September 1, 1849.

Parenthetically it is to be noticed that this event took place a considerable time after the first discovery of gold. It can in no sense be considered as a sequel to that fact. The numbers from the gold rush came in later. The constitutional convention was composed mainly of men who had previous interests in the country. They were representative of the time and place. The oldest delegate was fifty-three years and the youngest twenty-five years old. Fourteen were lawyers, fourteen were farmers, nine were merchants, five were soldiers, two were printers, one was a doctor, and one described himself as "a gentleman of elegant leisure."

The deliberations of this body are very interesting reading. Such a subject is usually dry in the extreme; but here we have men assembled from all over the world trying to piece together a form of government from the experiences of the different communities from which they originally came. Many Spanish Californians were represented on the floor. The different points brought up and discussed, in addition to those finally incorporated in the constitution, are both a valuable measure of the degree of intelligence at that time, and an indication of what men considered important in the problems of the day. The constitution itself was one of the best of the thirty-one state constitutions that then existed. Though almost every provision in it was copied from some other instrument, the choice was good. A provision prohibiting slavery was carried by a unanimous vote. When the convention adjourned, the new commonwealth was equipped with all the necessary machinery for regular government. [The constitution was ratified by popular vote, November 13, 1849; and the machinery of state government was at once set in motion, though the State was not admitted into the Union until September 9. 1850.]

It is customary to say that the discovery of gold made the State of California. As a matter of fact, it introduced into the history of California a new solvent, but it was in no sense a determining factor in either the acquisition or the assuring of the American hold. It must not be forgotten that a rising tide of American immigration had already set in. By 1845 the white population had increased to about eight thousand. At the close of hostilities it was estimated that the white population had increased to somewhere between twelve and fifteen thousand. Moreover this immigration, though established and constantly growing, was by no means top heavy. There was plenty of room in the north for the Americans, and they were settling there peaceably. Those who went south generally bought their land in due form. They and the Californians were getting on much better than is usual with conquering and conquered peoples.

But the discovery of gold upset all this orderly development. It wiped out the usual evolution. It not only swept aside at once the antiquated Mexican laws, but it submerged for the time being the first stirrings of the commonwealth toward due convention and legislation after the American pattern. It produced an interim wherein the only law was that evolved from men's consciences and the Anglo-Saxon instinct for order. It brought to shores remote from their native lands a cosmopolitan crew whose only thought was a fixed determination to undertake no new responsibilities. Each man was living for himself. He intended to get his own and to protect his own, and he cared very little for the difficulties of his neighbors. In other words, the discovery of gold offered California as the blank of a mint to receive the impress of a brand new civilization. And furthermore it gave to these men and, through them, to the world an impressive lesson that social responsibility can be evaded for a time, to be sure, but only for a time; and that at the last it must be taken up and the arrears must be paid.

Chapter Four: Gold

The discovery of gold—made, as everyone knows, by James Marshall, a foreman of Sutter's, engaged in building a sawmill for the Captain—came at a psychological time. [January 24, 1848, is the date usually given.] The Mexican War was just over and the adventurous spirits, unwilling to settle down, were looking for new excitement. Furthermore, the hard times of the Forties had blanketed the East with mortgages. Many sober communities were ready, deliberately and without excitement, to send their young men westward in the hope of finding a way out of their financial difficulties. The Oregon question, as has been already indicated, had aroused patriotism to such an extent that westward migration had become a sort of mental contagion.

It took some time for the first discoveries to leak out, and to be believed after they had gained currency. Even in California itself interest was rather tepid at first. Gold had been found in small quantities many years before, and only the actual sight of the metal in considerable weight could rouse men's imaginations to the blazing point.

Among the most enthusiastic protagonists was one Sam Brannan, who often appeared afterwards in the pages of Californian history. Brannan was a Mormon who had set out from New York with two hundred and fifty Mormons to try out the land of California as a possible refuge for the persecuted sect. That the westward migration of Mormons stopped at Salt Lake may well be due to the fact that on entering San Francisco Bay, Brannan found himself just too late. The American flag was already floating over the Presidio. Eye-witnesses say that Brannan dashed his hat to the deck, exclaiming, "There is that damned rag again." However, he proved an adaptable creature, for he and his Mormons landed nevertheless, and took up the industries of the country.

Brannan collected the usual tithes from these men, with the ostensible purpose of sending them on to the Church at Salt Lake. This, however, he consistently failed to do. One of the Mormons, on asking Sutter how long they should be expected to pay these tithes, received the answer,

"As long as you are fools enough to do so." But they did not remain fools very much longer, and Brannan found himself deprived of this source of revenue. On being dunned by Brigham Young for the tithes already collected, Brannan blandly resigned from the Church, still retaining the assets. With this auspicious beginning, aided by a burly, engaging personality, a coarse, direct manner that appealed to men, and an instinct for the limelight, he went far. Though there were a great many admirable traits in his character, people were forced to like him in spite of rather than because of them. His enthusiasm for any public agitation was always on tap.

In the present instance he rode down from Sutter's Fort, where he then had a store, bringing with him gold-dust and nuggets from the new placers.

"Gold! Gold! Gold from the American River!" shouted Brannan, as he strode down the street, swinging his hat in one hand and holding aloft the bottle of gold-dust in the other. This he displayed to the crowd that immediately gathered. With such a start, this new interest brought about a stampede that nearly depopulated the city.

The fever spread. People scrambled to the mines from all parts of the State. Practically every able-bodied man in the community, except the Spanish Californians, who as usual did not join this new enterprise with any unanimity, took at least a try at the diggings. Not only did they desert almost every sort of industry, but soldiers left the ranks and sailors the ships, so that often a ship was left in sole charge of its captain. All of American and foreign California moved to the foothills.

Then ensued the brief period so affectionately described in all literalness as the Arcadian Age. Men drank and gambled and enjoyed themselves in the rough manner of mining camps; but they were hardly ever drunken and in no instance dishonest. In all literalness the miners kept their gold-dust in tin cans and similar receptacles, on shelves, unguarded in tents or open cabins. Even quarrels and disorder were practically unknown. The communities were individualistic in the extreme, and yet, with the Anglo-Saxon love of order, they adopted rules and regulations and simple forms of government that proved entirely adequate to their needs. When the "good old days" are mentioned with the lingering regret associated with that phrase, the reference is to this brief period that came between the actual discovery and appreciation of gold and the influx from abroad that came in the following years.

This condition was principally due to the class of men concerned. The earliest miners were a very different lot from the majority of those who arrived in the next few years. They were mostly the original population, who had come out either as pioneers or in the government service. They included the discharged soldiers of Stevenson's regiment of New York Volunteers, who had been detailed for the war but who had arrived a little late, the so-called Mormon Battalion, Sam Brannan's immigrants, and those who had come as settlers since 1842. They were a rough lot with both the virtues and the defects of the pioneer. Nevertheless among their most marked characteristics were their honesty and their kindness.

Hittell gives an incident that illustrates the latter trait very well. "It was a little camp, the name of which is not given and perhaps is not important. The day was a hot one when a youth of sixteen came limping along, footsore, weary, hungry, and penniless. There were at least thirty robust miners at work in the ravine and it may well be believed they were cheerful, probably now and then joining in a chorus or laughing at a joke. The lad, as he saw and heard them, sat down upon the bank, his face telling the sad story of his misfortunes. Though he said nothing he was not unobserved. At length one of the miners, a stalwart fellow, pointing up to the poor fellow on the bank, exclaimed to his companions, 'Boys, I'll work an hour for that chap if you will.' All answered in the affirmative and picks and shovels were plied with even more activity than before. At the end of an hour a hundred dollars' worth of gold-dust was poured into his handkerchief. As this was done the miners who had crowded around the grateful boy made out a list of tools and said to him: 'You go now and buy these tools and come back. We'll have a good claim staked out for you; then you've got to paddle for yourself.'"

Another reason for this distinguished honesty was the extent and incredible richness of the diggings, combined with the firm belief that this richness would last forever and possibly increase. The first gold was often found actually at the roots of bushes, or could be picked out from the veins in the rocks by the aid of an ordinary hunting-knife. Such pockets were, to be sure, by no means numerous; but the miners did not know that. To them it seemed extremely possible that gold in such quantities was to be found almost anywhere for the mere seeking.

Authenticated instances are known of men getting ten, fifteen, twenty, and thirty thousand dollars within a week or ten days, without particularly hard work. Gold was so abundant it was much easier to dig it than to steal it, considering the risks attendant on the latter course. A story is told of a miner, while paying for something, dropping a small lump of gold worth perhaps two or three dollars. A bystander picked it up and offered it to him. The miner, without taking it, looked at the man with amazement, exclaiming: "Well, stranger, you are a curiosity. I guess you haven't been in the diggings long. You had better keep that lump for a sample."

These were the days of the red-shirted miner, of romance, of Arcadian simplicity, of clean, honest working under blue skies and beneath the warm California sun, of immense fortunes made quickly, of faithful "pardners," and all the rest. This life was so complete in all its elements that, as we look back upon it, we unconsciously give it a longer period than it actually occupied. It seems to be an epoch, as indeed it was; but it was an epoch of less than a single year, and it ended when the immigration from the world at large began.

The first news of the gold discovery filtered to the east in a roundabout fashion through vessels from the Sandwich Islands. A Baltimore paper published a short item. Everybody laughed at the rumor, for people were already beginning to discount California stories. But they remembered it. Romance, as ever, increases with the square of the distance; and this was a remote land. But soon there came an official letter written by Governor Mason to the War Department wherein he said that in his opinion, "There is more gold in the country drained by the Sacramento and San Joaquín rivers than would pay the cost of the late war with Mexico a hundred times over." The public immediately was alert.

And then, strangely enough, to give direction to the restless spirit seething beneath the surface of society, came a silly popular song. As has happened many times before and since, a great movement was set to the lilt of a commonplace melody. Minstrels started it; the public caught it up. Soon in every quarter of the world were heard the strains of *Oh, Susannah*! or rather the modification of it made to fit this case:

"I'll scrape the mountains clean, old girl,
I'll drain the rivers dry.
I'm off for California, Susannah, don't you cry.
Oh, Susannah, don't you cry for me,
I'm off to California with my wash bowl on my knee!"

The public mind already prepared for excitement by the stirring events of the past few years, but now falling into the doldrums of both monotonous and hard times, responded eagerly. Every man with a drop of red blood in his veins wanted to go to California. But the journey was a long one, and it cost a great deal of money, and there were such things as ties of family or business impossible to shake off. However, those who saw no immediate prospect of going often joined the curious clubs formed for the purpose of getting at least one or more of their members to the El Dorado. These clubs met once in so often, talked over details, worked upon each other's excitement even occasionally and officially sent some one of their members to the point of running amuck. Then he usually broke off all responsibilities and rushed headlong to the gold coast.

The most absurd ideas obtained currency. Stories did not lose in travel. A work entitled *Three Weeks in the Gold Mines*, written by a mendacious individual who signed himself H.I. Simpson, had a wide vogue. It is doubtful if the author had ever been ten miles from New York; but he wrote a marvelous and at the time convincing tale. According to his account, Simpson had only three weeks for a tour of the gold-fields, and considered ten days of the period was all he could spare the unimportant job of picking up gold. In the ten days, however, with no other implements than a pocket-knife, he accumulated fifty thousand dollars. The rest of the time he really preferred to travel about viewing the country! He condescended, however, to pick up incidental nuggets that happened to lie under his very footstep. Said one man to his friend: "I believe I'll go. I know most of this talk is wildly exaggerated, but I am sensible enough to discount all that sort of thing and to disbelieve absurd stories. I shan't go with the slightest notion of finding the thing true, but will be satisfied if I do reasonably well. In fact, if I don't pick up more than a hatful of gold a day I shall be perfectly satisfied."

Men's minds were full of strange positive knowledge, not only as to the extent of the goldmines, but also as to theory and practice of the actual mining. Contemporary writers tell us of the hundreds and hundreds of different strange machines invented for washing out the gold and actually carried around the Horn or over the Isthmus of Panama to San Francisco. They were of all types, from little pocket-sized affairs up to huge arrangements with windmill arms and wings. Their destination was inevitably the beach below the San Francisco settlement, where, half buried in the sand, torn by the trade winds, and looted for whatever of value might inhere in the metal parts, they rusted and disintegrated, a pathetic and grisly reminder of the futile greed of men.

Nor was this excitement confined to the eastern United States. In France itself lotteries were held, called, I believe, the *Lotteries of the Golden Ingot*. The holders of the winning tickets were given a trip to the gold-fields. A considerable number of French came over in that manner, so that life in California was then, as now, considerably leavened by Gallicism. Their ignorance of English together with their national clannishness caused them to stick together in communities.

They soon became known as *Keskydees*. Very few people knew why. It was merely the frontiersmen's understanding of the invariable French phrase *"Qu'est-ce *qu'il dit?"* In Great Britain, Norway, to a certain extent in Germany, South America, and even distant Australia, the adventurous and impecunious were pricking up their ears and laying their plans.

There were offered three distinct channels for this immigration. The first of these was by sailing around Cape Horn. This was a slow but fairly comfortable and reasonably safe route. It was never subject to the extreme overcrowding of the Isthmus route, and it may be dismissed in this paragraph. The second was by the overland route, of which there were several trails. The third was by the Isthmus of Panama. Each of these two is worth a chapter, and we shall take up the overland migration first.

Chapter Five: Across the Plains

The overland migration attracted the more hardy and experienced pioneers, and also those whose assets lay in cattle and farm equipment rather than in money. The majority came from the more western parts of the then United States, and therefore comprised men who had already some experience in pioneering. As far as the Mississippi or even Kansas these parties generally traveled separately or in small groups from a single locality. Before starting over the great plains, however, it became necessary to combine into larger bands for mutual aid and protection.

Such recognized meeting-points were therefore generally in a state of congestion. Thousands of people with their equipment and animals were crowded together in some river-bottom awaiting the propitious moment for setting forth.

The journey ordinarily required about five months, provided nothing untoward happened in the way of delay. A start in the spring therefore allowed the traveler to surmount the Sierra Nevada mountains before the first heavy snowfalls. One of the inevitable anxieties was whether or not this crossing could be safely accomplished. At first the migration was thoroughly orderly and successful. As the stories from California became more glowing, and as the fever for gold mounted higher, the pace accelerated.

A book by a man named Harlan, written in the County Farm to which his old age had brought him, gives a most interesting picture of the times. His party consisted of fourteen persons, one of whom, Harlan's grandmother, was then ninety years old and blind! There were also two very small children. At Indian Creek in Kansas they caught up with the main body of immigrants and soon made up their train. He says: "We proceeded very happily until we reached the South Platte. Every night we young folks had a dance on the green prairie." Game abounded, the party was in good spirits and underwent no especial hardships, and the Indian troubles furnished only sufficient excitement to keep the men interested and alert. After leaving Salt Lake, however, the passage across the desert suddenly loomed up as a terrifying thing. "We started on our passage over this desert in the early morning, trailed all next day and all night, and on the morning of the third day our guide told us that water was still twenty-five miles away. William Harlan here lost his seven yoke of oxen. The man who was in charge of them went to sleep, and the cattle turned back and recrossed the desert or perhaps died there.... Next day I started early and drove till dusk, as I wished to tire the cattle so that they would lie down and give me a chance to sleep. They would rest for two or three hours and then try to go back home to their former range." The party won through, however, and descended into the smiling valleys of California, ninety-year-old lady and all.

These parties which were hastily got together for the mere purpose of progress soon found that they must have some sort of government to make the trip successful. A leader was generally elected to whom implicit obedience was supposed to be accorded. Among independent and hotheaded men quarrels were not infrequent. A rough sort of justice was, however, invoked by vote of the majority. Though a "split of blankets" was not unknown, usually the party went through under one leadership. Fortunate were those who possessed experienced men as leaders, or who in hiring the services of one of the numerous plains guides obtained one of genuine experience. Inexperience and graft were as fatal then as now. It can well be imagined what disaster could descend upon a camping party in a wilderness such as the Old West, amidst the enemies which that wilderness supported. It is bad enough today when inexperienced people go to camp by a lake near a farmhouse. Moreover, at that time everybody was in a hurry, and many suspected that the other man was trying to obtain an advantage.

Hittell tells of one ingenious citizen who, in trying to keep ahead of his fellow immigrants as he hurried along, had the bright idea of setting on fire and destroying the dry grass in order to retard the progress of the parties behind. Grass was scarce enough in the best circumstances, and the burning struck those following with starvation. He did not get very far, however, before he was caught by a posse who mounted their best horses for pursuit. They shot him from his saddle and turned back. This attempt at monopoly was thus nipped in the bud.

Probably there would have been more of this sort of thing had it not been for the constant menace of the Indians. The Indian attack on the immigrant train has become so familiar through Wild West shows and so-called literature that it is useless to redescribe it here. Generally the object was merely the theft of horses, but occasionally a genuine attack, followed in case of success by massacre, took place. An experience of this sort did a great deal of good in holding together not only the parties attacked, but also those who afterwards heard of the attempt.

There was, however, another side to the shield, a very encouraging and cheerful side. For example, some good-hearted philanthropist established a kind of reading-room and post-office in the desert near the headwaters of the Humboldt River. He placed it in a natural circular wall of rock by the road, shaded by a lone tree. The original founder left a lot of newspapers on a stone seat inside the wall with a written notice to "Read and leave them for others."

Many trains, well equipped, well formed, well led, went through without trouble--indeed, with real pleasure. Nevertheless the overwhelming testimony is on the other side. Probably this was due in large part to the irritability that always seizes the mind of the tenderfoot when he is confronted by wilderness conditions. A man who is a perfectly normal and agreeable citizen in his own environment becomes a suspicious half-lunatic when placed in circumstances uncomfortable and unaccustomed. It often happened that people were obliged to throw things away in order to lighten their loads. When this necessity occurred, they generally seemed to take an extraordinary delight in destroying their property rather than in leaving it for anybody else who might come along. Hittell tells us that sugar was often ruined by having turpentine poured over it, and flour was mixed with salt and dirt; wagons were burned; clothes were torn into shreds and tatters. All of this destruction was senseless and useless, and was probably only a blind and instinctive reaction against hardships.

Those hardships were considerable. It is estimated that during the height of the overland migration in the spring of 1849 no less than fifty thousand people started out. The wagon trains followed almost on one another's heels, so hot was the pace. Not only did the travelers wish to get to the Sierras before the snows blocked the passes, not only were they eager to enter the gold mines, but they were pursued by the specter of cholera in the concentration camps along the Mississippi Valley. This scourge devastated these gatherings. It followed the men across the plains like some deadly wild beast, and was shaken off only when the high clear climate of desert altitude was eventually reached.

But the terrible part of the journey began with the entrance into the great deserts, like that of the Humboldt Sink. There the conditions were almost beyond belief.

Thousands were left behind, fighting starvation, disease, and the loss of cattle. Women who had lost their husbands from the deadly cholera went staggering on without food or water, leading their children. The trail was literally lined with dead animals. Often in the middle of the desert could be seen the camps of death, the wagons drawn in a circle, the dead animals tainting the air, every living human being crippled from scurvy and other diseases. There was no fodder for the cattle, and very little water The loads had to be lightened almost every mile by the discarding of valuable goods. Many of the immigrants who survived the struggle reached the goal in an impoverished condition.

The road was bordered with an almost unbroken barrier of abandoned wagons, old mining implements, clothes, provisions, and the like. As the cattle died, the problem of merely continuing the march became worse. Often the rate of progress was not more than a mile every two or three hours. Each mile had to be relayed back and forth several times. And when this desert had sapped their strength, they came at last to the Sink itself, with its long white fields of alkali with drifts of ashes across them, so soft that the cattle sank half-way to their bellies. The dust was fine and light and rose chokingly; the sun was strong and fierce. All but the strongest groups of pioneers seemed to break here.

The retreats became routs. Each one put out for himself with what strength he had left. The wagons were emptied of everything but the barest necessities. At every stop some animal fell in the traces and had to be cut out of the yoke. If a wagon came to a full stop, it was abandoned. The animals were detached and driven forward. And when at last they reached the Humboldt River itself, they found it almost impossible to ford. The best feed lay on the other side. In the distance the high and forbidding ramparts of the Sierra Nevadas reared themselves.

One of these Forty-niners, Delano, a man of some distinction in the later history of the mining communities, says that five men drowned themselves in the Humboldt River in one day out of sheer discouragement.

He says that he had to save the lives of his oxen by giving Indians fifteen dollars to swim the river and float some grass across to him. And with weakened cattle, discouraged hearts, no provisions, the travelers had to tackle the high rough road that led across the mountains.

Of course, the picture just drawn is of the darkest aspect. Some trains there were under competent pioneers who knew their job; who were experienced in wilderness travel; who understood better than to chase madly away after every cut-off reported by irresponsible trappers; who comprehended the handling and management of cattle; who, in short, knew wilderness travel. These came through with only the ordinary hardships.

But take it all in all, the overland trail was a trial by fire. One gets a notion of its deadliness from the fact that over five thousand people died of cholera alone. The trail was marked throughout its length by the shallow graves of those who had succumbed. He who arrived in California was a different person from the one who had started from the East. Experience had even in so short a time fused his elements into something new. This alteration must not be forgotten when we turn once more to the internal affairs of the new commonwealth.

Chapter Six: The Mormons

In the westward overland migration the Salt Lake Valley Mormons played an important part. These strange people had but recently taken up their abode in the desert. That was a fortunate circumstance, as their necessities forced them to render an aid to the migration that in better days would probably have been refused.

The founder of the Mormon Church, Joseph Smith, Jr., came from a commonplace family.

Apparently its members were ignorant and superstitious. They talked much of hidden treasure and of supernatural means for its discovery. They believed in omens, signs, and other superstitions. As a boy Joseph had been shrewd enough and superstitious enough to play this trait up for all it was worth. He had a magic peep-stone and a witch-hazel divining-rod that he manipulated so skillfully as to cause other boys and even older men to dig for him as he wished. He seemed to delight in tricking his companions in various ways, by telling fortunes, reeling off tall yarns, and posing as one possessed of occult knowledge.

According to Joseph's autobiography, the discovery of the Mormon Bible happened in this wise: on the night of September 21, 1823, a vision fell upon him; the angel Moroni appeared and directed him to a cave on the hillside; in this cave he found some gold plates, on which were inscribed strange characters, written in what Smith described as "reformed Egyptian"; they were undecipherable except by the aid of a pair of magic peep-stones named Urim and Thummim, delivered him for the purpose by the angel at Palmyra; looking through the hole in these peep-stones, he was able to interpret the gold plates. This was the skeleton of the story embellished by later ornamentation in the way of golden breastplates, two stones bright and shining, golden plates united at the back by rings, the Sword of Laban, square stone boxes, cemented clasps, invisible blows, suggestions of Satan, and similar mummery born from the quickened imagination of a zealot.

Smith succeeded in interesting one Harris to act as his amanuensis in his interpretation of these books of Mormon. The future prophet sat behind a screen with the supposed gold plates in his hat. He dictated through the stones Urim and Thummim. With a keen imagination and natural aptitude for the strikingly dramatic, he was able to present formally his ritual, tabernacle, holy of holies, priesthood and tithings, constitution and councils, blood atonement, anointment, twelve apostles, miracles, his spiritual manifestations and revelations, all in reminiscence of the religious tenets of many lands.

Such religious movements rise and fall at periodic intervals. Sometimes they are never heard of outside the small communities of their birth; at other times they arise to temporary nation-wide importance, but they are unlucky either in leadership or environment and so perish.

The Mormon Church, however, was fortunate in all respects. Smith was in no manner a successful leader, but he made a good prophet. He was strong physically, was a great wrestler, and had an abundance of good nature; he was personally popular with the type of citizen with whom he was thrown. He could impress the ignorant mind with the reality of his revelations and the potency of his claims. He could impress the more intelligent, but half unscrupulous, half fanatical minds of the leaders with the power of his idea and the opportunities offered for leadership.

Two men of the latter type were Parley P. Pratt and Sidney Rigdon. The former was of the narrow, strong, fanatic type; the latter had the cool constructive brain that gave point, direction, and consistency to the Mormon system of theology. Had it not been for such leaders and others like them, it is quite probable that the Smith movement would have been lost like hundreds of others. That Smith himself lasted so long as the head of the Church, with the powers and perquisites of that position, can be explained by the fact that, either by accident or shrewd design, his position before the unintelligent masses had been made impregnable.

If it was not true that Joseph Smith had received the golden plates from an angel and had translated them—again in with the assistance of an angel—and had received from heaven the revelations vouchsafed from time to time for the explicit guidance of the Church in moral, temporal, and spiritual matters, then there was no Book of Mormon, no new revelation, no Mormon Church. The dethronement of Smith meant that there could be no successor to Smith, for there would be nothing to which to succeed. The whole church structure must crumble with him.

The time was psychologically right. Occasionally a contagion of religious need seems to sweep the country. People demand manifestations and signs, and will flock to any who can promise them. To this class the Book of Mormon, with its definite sort of mysticism, appealed strongly. The promises of a new Zion were concrete; the power was centralized, so that people who had heretofore been floundering in doubt felt they could lean on authority, and shake off the personal responsibility that had weighed them down. The Mormon communities grew fast, and soon began to send out proselyting missionaries. England was especially a fruitful field for these missionaries. The great manufacturing towns were then at their worst, containing people desperately ignorant, superstitious, and so deeply poverty-stricken that the mere idea of owning land of their own seemed to them the height of affluence. Three years after the arrival of the missionaries the general conference reported 4019 converts in England alone. These were good material in the hands of strong, fanatical, or unscrupulous leaders. They were religious enthusiasts, of course, who believed they were coming to a real city of Zion. Most of them were in debt to the Church for the price of their passage, and their expenses. They were dutiful in their acceptance of miracles, signs, and revelations. The more intelligent among them realized that, having come so far and invested in the enterprise their all, it was essential that they accept wholly the discipline and authority of the Church.

Before their final migration to Utah, the Mormons made three ill-fated attempts to found the city of Zion, first in Ohio, then in western Missouri, and finally, upon their expulsion from Missouri, at Nauvoo in Illinois. In every case they both inspired and encountered opposition and sometimes persecution. As the Mormons increased in power, they became more self-sufficient and arrogant. They at first presumed to dictate politically, and then actually began to consider themselves a separate political entity. One of their earliest pieces of legislation, under the act incorporating the city of Nauvoo, was an ordinance to protect the inhabitants of the Mormon communities from all outside legal processes. No writ for the arrest of any Mormon inhabitants of any Mormon city could be executed until it had received the mayor's approval. By way of a mild and adequate penalty, anyone violating this ordinance was to be imprisoned for life with no power of pardon in the governor without the mayor's consent.

Of course this was a welcome opportunity for the lawless and desperate characters of the surrounding country. They became Mormon to a man.

Under the shield of Mormon protection they could steal and raid to their heart's content. Land speculators also came into the Church, and bought land in the expectation that New Zion property would largely rise. Banking grew somewhat frantic. Complaints became so bitter that even the higher church authorities were forced to take cognizance of the practices.

In 1840 Smith himself said: "We are no longer at war, and you must stop stealing. When the right time comes, we will go in force and take the whole State of Missouri. It belongs to us as our inheritance, but I want no more petty stealing. A man that will steal petty articles from his enemies will, when occasion offers, steal from his brethren too. Now I command you that have stolen must steal no more."

At Nauvoo, on the eastern bank of the Mississippi, they built a really pretentious and beautiful city, and all but completed a temple that was, from every account, creditable. However, their arrogant relations with their neighbors and the extreme isolation in which they held themselves soon earned them the dislike and distrust of those about them. The practice of polygamy had begun, although even to the rank and file of the Mormons themselves the revelation commanding it was as yet unknown.

Still, rumors had leaked forth. The community, already severely shocked in its economic sense, was only too ready to be shocked in its moral sense, as is the usual course of human nature. The rather wild vagaries of the converts, too, aroused distrust and disgust in the sober minds of the western pioneers. At religious meetings converts would often arise to talk in gibberish—utterly nonsensical gibberish. This was called a "speaking with tongues," and could be translated by the speaker or a bystander in any way he saw fit, without responsibility for the saying. This was an easy way of calling a man names without standing behind it, so to speak. The congregation saw visions, read messages on stones picked up in the field—messages which disappeared as soon as interpreted. They had fits in meetings, they chased balls of fire through the fields, they saw wonderful lights in the air, in short they went through all the hysterical vagaries formerly seen also in the Methodist revivals under John Wesley.

Turbulence outside was accompanied by turbulence within. Schisms occurred. Branches were broken off from the Church. The great temporal power and wealth to which, owing to the obedience and docility of the rank and file, the leaders had fallen practically sole heirs, had gone to their heads. The Mormon Church gave every indication of breaking up into disorganized smaller units, when fortunately for it the prophet Joseph Smith and his brother Hyrum were killed by a mob. This martyrdom consolidated the church body once more; and before disintegrating influences could again exert themselves, the reins of power were seized by the strong hand of a remarkable man, Brigham Young, who thrust aside the logical successor, Joseph Smith's son.

Young was an uneducated man, but with a deep insight into human nature. A shrewd practical ability and a rugged intelligence, combined with absolute cold-blooded unscrupulousness in attaining his ends, were qualities amply sufficient to put Young in the front rank of the class of people who composed the Mormon Church. He early established a hierarchy of sufficient powers so that always he was able to keep the strong men of the Church loyal to the idea he represented. He paid them well, both in actual property and in power that was dearer to them than property. Furthermore, whether or not he originated polygamy, he not only saw at once its uses in increasing the population of the new state and in taking care of the extra women such fanatical religions always attract, but also, more astutely, he realized that the doctrine of polygamy would set his people apart from all other people, and probably call down upon them the direct opposition of the Federal Government. A feeling of persecution, opposition, and possible punishment were all potent to segregate the Mormon Church from the rest of humanity and to assure its coherence. Further, he understood thoroughly the results that can be obtained by cooperation of even mediocre people under able leadership. He placed his people apart by thoroughly impressing upon their minds the idea of their superiority to the rest of the world. They were the chosen people, hitherto scattered, but now at last gathered together. His followers had just the degree of intelligence necessary to accept leadership gracefully and to rejoice in a supposed superiority because of a sense of previous inferiority.

This ductile material Brigham welded to his own forms. He was able to assume consistently an appearance of uncouth ignorance in order to retain his hold over his uncultivated flock. He delivered vituperative, even obscene sermons, which may still be read in his collected works. But he was able also on occasions, as when addressing agents of the Federal Government or other outsiders whom he wished to impress, to write direct and dignified English. He was resourceful in obtaining control over the other strong men of his Church; but by his very success he was blinded to due proportions. There can be little doubt that at one time he thought he could defy the United States by force of arms. He even maintained an organization called the Danites, sometimes called the Destroying Angels, who carried out his decrees. [The Mormon Church has always denied the existence of any such organization; but the weight of evidence is against the Church. In one of his discourses, Young seems inadvertently to have admitted the existence of the Danites. The organization dates from the sojourn of the Mormons in Missouri. See Linn, *The Story of the Mormons*, pp. 189-192.]

Brigham could welcome graciously and leave a good impression upon important visitors. He was not a good business man, however, and almost every enterprise he directly undertook proved to be a complete or partial failure. He did the most extraordinarily stupid things, as, for instance, when he planned the so-called Cottonwood Canal, the mouth of which was ten feet higher than its source! Nevertheless he had sense to utilize the business ability of other men, and was a good accumulator of properties. His estate at his death was valued at between two and three million dollars. This was a pretty good saving for a pioneer who had come into the wilderness without a cent of his own, who had always spent lavishly, and who had supported a family of over twenty wives and fifty children—all this without a salary as an officer. Tithes were brought to him personally, and he rendered no accounting. He gave the strong men of his hierarchy power and opportunity, played them against each other to keep his own lead, and made holy any of their misdeeds which were not directed against himself.

The early months of 1846 witnessed a third Mormon exodus. Driven out of Illinois, these Latter-day Saints crossed the Mississippi in organized bands, with Council Bluffs as their first objective. Through the winter and spring some fifteen thousand Mormons with three thousand wagons found their way from camp to camp, through snow, ice, and mud, over the weary stretch of four hundred miles to the banks of the Missouri. The epic of this westward migration is almost biblical. Hardship brought out the heroic in many characters. Like true American pioneers, they adapted themselves to circumstances with fortitude and skill.

Linn says: "When a halt occurred, a shoemaker might be seen looking for a stone to serve as a lap-stone in his repair work, or a gunsmith mending a rifle, or a weaver at a wheel or loom. The women learned that the jolting wagons would churn their milk, and when a halt occurred it took them but a short time to heat an oven hollowed out of the hillside, in which to bake the bread already raised."

Colonel Kane says that he saw a piece of cloth, the wool for which was sheared, dyed, spun, and woven, during the march.

After a winter of sickness and deprivation in camps along "Misery Bottom," as they called the river flats, during which malaria carried off hundreds, Brigham Young set out with a pioneer band of a hundred and fifty to find a new Zion. Toward the end of July, this expedition by design or chance entered Salt Lake Valley. At sight of the lake glistening in the sun, "Each of us," wrote one of the party, "without saying a word to the other, instinctively, as if by inspiration, raised our hats from our heads, and then, swinging our hats, shouted, 'Hosannah to God and the Lamb!'"

Meantime the first emigration from winter quarters was under way, and in the following spring Young conducted a train of eight hundred wagons across the plains to the great valley where a city of adobe and log houses was already building. The new city was laid off into numbered lots. The Presidency had charge of the distribution of these lots. You may be sure they did not reserve the worst for their use, nor did they place about themselves undesirable neighbors. Immediately after the assignments had been made, various people began at once to speculate in buying and selling according to the location. The spiritual power immediately anathematized this. No one was permitted to trade over property. Any sales were made on a basis of the first cost plus the value of the improvement. A community admirable in almost every way was improvised as though by magic. Among themselves the Mormons were sober, industrious, God-fearing, peaceful. Their difficulties with the nation were yet to come.

Throughout the year, 1848, the weather was propitious for ploughing and sowing. Before the crops could be gathered, however, provisions ran so low that the large community was in actual danger of starvation. Men were reduced to eating skins of slaughtered animals, the raw hides from the roofs of houses, and even a wild root dug by the miserable Ute Indians. To cap the climax, when finally the crops ripened, they were attacked by an army of crickets that threatened to destroy them utterly. Prayers of desperation were miraculously answered by a flight of white sea-gulls that destroyed the invader and saved the crop. Since then this miracle has been many times repeated.

It was in August, 1849, that the first gold rush began. Some of Brannan's company from California had already arrived with samples of gold-dust. Brigham Young was too shrewd not to discourage all mining desires on the part of his people, and he managed to hold them. The Mormons never did indulge in gold-mining. But the samples served to inflame the ardor of the immigrants from the east. Their one desire at once became to lighten their loads so that they could get to the diggings in the shortest possible time. Then the Mormons began to reap their harvest. Animals worth only twenty-five or thirty dollars would bring two hundred dollars in exchange for goods brought in by the travelers. For a light wagon the immigrants did not hesitate to offer three or four heavy ones, and sometimes a yoke of oxen to boot. Such very desirable things to a new community as sheeting, or spades and shovels, since the miners were overstocked, could be had for almost nothing. Indeed, everything, except coffee and sugar, was about half the wholesale rate in the East.

The profit to the Mormons from this migration was even greater in 1850. The gold-seeker sometimes paid as high as a dollar a pound for flour; and, conversely, as many of the wayfarers started out with heavy loads of mining machinery and miscellaneous goods, as is the habit of the tenderfoot camper even unto this day, they had to sell at the buyers' prices. Some of the enterprising miners had even brought large amounts of goods for sale at a hoped-for profit in California.

At Salt Lake City, however, the information was industriously circulated that shiploads of similar, merchandise were on their way round the Horn, and consequently the would-be traders often sacrificed their own stock. [Linn, *The Story of the Mormons*, 406.]

This friendly condition could not, of course, long obtain. Brigham Young's policy of segregation was absolutely opposed to permanent friendly relations. The immigrants on the other hand were violently prejudiced against the Mormon faith. The valley of the Salt Lake seemed to be just the psychological point for the breaking up into fragments of the larger companies that had crossed the plains. The division of property on these separations sometimes involved a considerable amount of difficulty. The disputants often applied to the Mormon courts for decision. Somebody was sure to become dissatisfied and to accuse the courts of undue influence. Rebellion against the decision brought upon them the full force of civil power. For contempt of court they were most severely fined. The fields of the Mormons were imperfectly fenced; the cattle of the immigrants were very numerous. Trespass cases brought heavy remuneration, the value being so much greater for damages than in the States that it often looked to the stranger like an injustice. A protest would be taken before a bishop who charged costs for his decision. An unreasonable prejudice against the Mormons often arose from these causes. On the other hand there is no doubt that the immigrants often had right on their side. Not only were the Mormons human beings, with the usual qualities of love of gain and desire to take advantage of their situation; but, further, they belonged to a sect that fostered the belief that they were superior to the rest of mankind, and that it was actually meritorious to "spoil the Philistines."

Many gold-diggers who started out with a complete outfit finished their journey almost on foot. Some five hundred of these people got together later in California and compared notes. Finally they drew up a series of affidavits to be sent back home. A petition was presented to Congress charging that many immigrants had been murdered by the Mormons; that, when members of the Mormon community became dissatisfied and tried to leave, they were subdued and killed; that a two per cent tax on the property was levied on those immigrants compelled to stay through the winter; that justice was impossible to obtain in the Mormon courts; that immigrants' mail was opened and destroyed; and that all Mormons were at best treasonable in sentiment. Later the breach between the Mormons and the Americans became more marked, until it culminated in the atrocious Mountain Meadows massacre, which was probably only one of several similar but lesser occurrences. These things, however, are outside of our scope, as they occurred later in history. For the moment, it is only necessary to note that it was extremely fortunate for the gold immigrants, not only that the half-way station had been established by the Mormons, but also that the necessities of the latter forced them to adopt a friendly policy. By the time open enmity had come, the first of the rush had passed and other routes had been well established.

Chapter Seven: The Way by Panama

Of the three roads to California that by Panama was the most obvious, the shortest, and therefore the most crowded. It was likewise the most expensive. To the casual eye this route was also the easiest. You got on a ship in New York, you disembarked for a very short land journey, you re-embarked on another ship, and landed at San Francisco. This route therefore attracted the more unstable elements of society. The journey by the plains took a certain grim determination and courage; that by Cape Horn, a slow and persistent patience.

The route by the Isthmus, on the other hand, allured the impatient, the reckless, and those who were unaccustomed to and undesirous of hardships. Most of the gamblers and speculators, for example, as well as the cheaper politicians, went by Panama.

In October, 1848, the first steamship of the Pacific Steamship Company began her voyage from New York to Panama and San Francisco, and reached her destination toward the end of February. On the Atlantic every old tub that could be made to float so far was pressed into service. Naturally there were many more vessels on the Atlantic side than on the Pacific side, and the greatest congestion took place at Panama. Every man was promised by the shipping agent a through passage, but the shipping agent was careful to remain in New York.

The overcrowded ships were picturesque though uncomfortable. They were crowded to the guards with as miscellaneous a lot of passengers as were ever got together. It must be remembered that they were mostly young men in the full vigor of youth and thoroughly imbued with the adventurous spirit. It must be remembered again, if the reader can think back so far in his own experience, that youth of that age loves to deck itself out both physically and mentally in the trappings of romance. Almost every man wore a red shirt, a slouch hat, a repeating pistol, and a bowie-knife; and most of them began at once to grow beards. They came from all parts of the country. The lank Maine Yankee elbowed the tall, sallow, black-haired Southerner. Social distinctions soon fell away and were forgotten. No one could tell by speech, manners, or dress whether a man's former status was lawyer, physician, or roustabout. The days were spent in excited discussions of matters pertaining to the new country and the theory and practice of gold-mining. Only two things were said to be capable of breaking in on this interminable palaver. One was dolphins and the other the meal-gong. When dolphins appeared, each passenger promptly rushed to the side of the ship and discharged his revolver in a fusillade that was usually harmless. Meal time always caught the majority unawares. They tumbled and jostled down the companionway only to find that the wise and forethoughtful had preempted every chair. There was very little quarreling. A holiday spirit seemed to pervade the crowd. Everybody was more or less elevated in mood and everybody was imbued with the same spirit of comradeship in adventure.

But with the sight of shore, the low beach, and the round high bluffs with the castle atop that meant Chagres, this comradeship rather fell apart. Soon a landing was to be made and transportation across the Isthmus had to be obtained. Men at once became rivals for prompt service. Here, for the first time, the owners of the weird mining-machines already described found themselves at a disadvantage, while those who carried merely the pick, shovel, and small personal equipment were enabled to make a flying start. On the beach there was invariably an immense wrangle over the hiring of boats to go up the river. These were a sort of dug-out with small decks in the bow and in the stern, and with low roofs of palmetto leaves amidships. The fare to Cruces was about fifteen dollars a man. Nobody was in a hurry but the Americans.

Chagres was a collection of cane huts on level ground, with a swamp at the back. Men and women clad in a single cotton garment lay about smoking cigars. Naked and pot-bellied children played in the mud. On the threshold of the doors, in the huts, fish, bullock heads, hides, and carrion were strewn, all in a state of decomposition, while in the rear was the jungle and a lake of stagnant water with a delicate bordering of greasy blue mud. There was but one hotel, called the Crescent City, which boasted of no floor and no food. The newcomers who were unsupplied with provisions had to eat what they could pick up. Unlearned as yet in tropical ways, they wasted a tremendous lot of nervous energy in trying to get the natives started. The natives, calm in the consciousness that there was plenty of demand, refused to be hurried. Many of the travelers, thinking that they had closed a bargain, returned from sightseeing only to find their boat had disappeared. The only safe way was to sit in the canoe until it actually started.

With luck they got off late in the afternoon, and made ten or twelve miles to Gatun. The journey up the lazy tropical river was exciting and interesting. The boatmen sang, the tropic forests came down to the banks with their lilies, shrubs, mangoes, cocos, sycamores, palms; their crimson, purple, and yellow blossoms; their bananas with torn leaves; their butterflies and paroquets; their streamers and vines and scarlet flowers. It was like a vision of fairyland.

Gatun was a collection of bamboo huts, inhabited mainly by fleas. One traveler tells of attempting to write in his journal, and finding the page covered with fleas before he had inscribed a dozen words. The gold seekers slept in hammocks, suspended at such a height that the native dogs found them most convenient back-scratchers. The fleas were not inactive. On all sides the natives drank, sang, and played monte. It generally rained at night, and the flimsy huts did little to keep out the wet. Such things went far to take away the first enthusiasm and to leave the travelers in rather a sad and weary-eyed state.

By the third day the river narrowed and became swifter. With luck the voyagers reached Gorgona on a high bluff. This was usually the end of the river journey. Most people bargained for Cruces six miles beyond, but on arrival decided that the Gorgona trail would be less crowded, and with unanimity went ashore there. Here the bargaining had to be started all over again, this time for mules. Here also the demand far exceeded the supply, with the usual result of arrogance, indifference, and high prices. The difficult ride led at first through a dark deep wood in clay soil that held water in every depression, seamed with steep eroded ravines and diversified by low passes over projecting spurs of a chain of mountains. There the monkeys and parrots furnished the tropical atmosphere, assisted somewhat by innumerable dead mules along the trail.

Vultures sat in every tree waiting for more things to happen. The trail was of the consistency of very thick mud. In this mud the first mule had naturally left his tracks; the next mules trod carefully in the first mule's footprints, and all subsequent mules did likewise. The consequence was a succession of narrow deep holes in the clay into which an animal sank half-way to the shoulder. No power was sufficient to make these mules step anywhere else. Each hole was full of muddy water. When the mule inserted his hoof, water spurted out violently as though from a squirt-gun. Walking was simply impossible.

All this was merely adventure for the young, strong, and healthy; but the terrible part of the Panama Trail was the number of victims claimed by cholera and fever. The climate and the unwonted labor brought to the point of exhaustion men unaccustomed to such exertions. They lay flat by the trail as though dead. Many actually did die either from the jungle fever or the yellow-jack. The universal testimony of the times is that this horseback journey seemed interminable; and many speak of being immensely cheered when their Indian stopped, washed his feet in a wayside mudhole, and put on his pantaloons. That indicated the proximity, at last, of the city of Panama.

It was a quaint old place. The two-story wooden houses with corridor and verandah across the face of the second story, painted in bright colors, leaned crazily out across the streets. Narrow and mysterious alleys led between them. Ancient cathedrals and churches stood gray with age before the grass-grown plazas. In the outskirts were massive masonry ruins of great buildings, convents, and colleges, some of which had never been finished. The immense blocks lay about the ground in confusion, covered by thousands of little plants, or soared against the sky in broken arches and corridors. But in the body of the town, the old picturesque houses had taken on a new and temporary smartness which consisted mostly of canvas signs. The main street was composed of hotels, eating-houses, and assorted hells. At times over a thousand men were there awaiting transportation. Some of them had been waiting a long time, and had used up all their money. They were broke and desperate. A number of American gambling-houses were doing business, and of course the saloons were much in evidence. Foreigners kept two of the three hotels; Americans ran the gambling joints; French and Germans kept the restaurants. The natives were content to be interested but not entirely idle spectators. There was a terrible amount of sickness aggravated by American quack remedies. Men rejoiced or despaired according to their dispositions. Every once in a while a train of gold bullion would start back across the Isthmus with mule-loads of huge gold bars, so heavy that they were safe, for no one could carry them off to the jungle.

On the other hand there were some returning Californians, drunken and wretched. They delighted in telling with grim joy of the disappointments of the diggings. But probably the only people thoroughly unhappy were the steamship officials. These men had to bear the brunt of disappointment, broken promises, and savage recrimination, if means for going north were not very soon forthcoming.

Every once in a while some ship, probably an old tub, would come wallowing to anchor at the nearest point, some eleven miles from the city. Then the raid for transportation took place all over again. There was a limited number of small boats for carrying purposes, and these were pounced on at once by ten times the number they could accommodate. Ships went north scandalously overcrowded and underprovisioned.

Mutinies were not infrequent. It took a good captain to satisfy everybody, and there were many bad ones. Some men got so desperate that, with a touching ignorance of geography, they actually started out in small boats to row to the north. Others attempted the overland route. It may well be believed that the reaction from all this disappointment and delay lifted the hearts of these argonauts when they eventually sailed between the Golden Gates.

This confusion, of course, was worse at the beginning. Later the journey was to some extent systematized. The Panama route subsequently became the usual and fashionable way to travel. The ship companies learned how to handle and treat their patrons. In fact, it was said that every jewelry shop in San Francisco carried a large stock of fancy silver speaking-trumpets because of the almost invariable habit of presenting one of these to the captain of the ship by his grateful passengers. One captain swore that he possessed eighteen of them!

Chapter Eight: The Diggings

The two streams of immigrants, by sea and overland, thus differed, on the average, in kind. They also landed in the country at different points. The overlanders were generally absorbed before they reached San Francisco. They arrived first at Fort Sutter, whence they distributed themselves; or perhaps they even stopped at one or another of the diggings on their way in.

Of those coming by sea all landed at San Francisco. A certain proportion of the younger and more enthusiastic set out for the mines, but only after a few days had given them experience of the new city and had impressed them with at least a subconscious idea of opportunity. Another certain proportion, however, remained in San Francisco without attempting the mines. These were either men who were discouraged by pessimistic tales, men who had sickened of the fever, or more often men who were attracted by the big opportunities for wealth which the city then afforded. Thus at once we have two different types to consider, the miner and the San Franciscan.

The mines were worked mostly by young men. They journeyed up to the present Sacramento either by river-boats or afoot. Thence they took their outfits into the diggings. It must have seemed a good deal like a picnic. The goal was near; rosy hope had expanded to fill the horizon; breathless anticipation pervaded them—a good deal like a hunting-party starting off in the freshness of the dawn.

The diggings were generally found at the bottoms of the deep river-beds and ravines. Since trails, in order to avoid freshets and too many crossings of the water-courses, took the higher shoulder of the hill, the newcomer ordinarily looked down upon his first glimpse of the mines.

The sight must have been busy and animated. The miners dressed in bright-colored garments, and dug themselves in only to the waist or at most to the shoulders before striking bed rock, so that they were visible as spots of gaudy color. The camps were placed on the hillsides or little open flats, and occasionally were set in the bed of a river. They were composed of tents, and of rough log or bark structures.

The newcomers did not spend much time in establishing themselves comfortably or luxuriously. They were altogether too eager to get at the actual digging. There was an immense excitement of the gamble in it all.

A man might dig for days without adequate results and then of a sudden run into a rich pocket. Or he might pan out an immense sum within the first ten minutes of striking his pick to earth. No one could tell. The fact that the average of all the days and all the men amounted to very little more than living wages was quite lost to sight.

At first the methods were very crude. One man held a coarse screen of willow branches which he shook continuously above an ordinary cooking pot, while his partner slowly shovelled earth over this impromptu sieve. When the pots were filled with siftings, they were carried to the river, where they were carefully submerged, and the contents were stirred about with sticks. The light earth was thus flowed over the rims of the pots. The residue was then dried, and the lighter sand was blown away. The result was gold, though of course with a strong mixture of foreign substance.

The pan miners soon followed; and the cradle or rocker with its riffle-board was not long delayed. The digging was free. At first it was supposed that a new holding should not be started within fifteen feet of one already in operation.

Later, claims of a definite size were established. A camp, however, made its own laws in regard to this and other matters.

Most of the would-be miners at first rather expected to find gold lying on the surface of the earth, and were very much disappointed to learn that they actually had to dig for it. Moreover, digging in the boulders and gravel, under the terrific heat of the California sun in midsummer, was none too easy; and no matter how rich the diggings averaged—short of an actual bonanza—the miner was disappointed in his expectations.

One man is reported saying: "They tell me I can easily make there eleven hundred dollars a day. You know I am not easily moved by such reports. I shall be satisfied if I make three hundred dollars per day."

Travelers of the time comment on the contrast between the returning stream of discouraged and disgruntled men and the cheerfulness of the lot actually digging. Nobody had any scientific system to go on. Often a divining-rod was employed to determine where to dig. Many stories were current of accidental finds; as when one man, tiring of waiting for his dog to get through digging out a ground squirrel, pulled the animal out by the tail, and with it a large nugget. Another story is told of a sailor who asked some miners resting at noon where he could dig and as a joke was directed to a most improbable side hill. He obeyed the advice, and uncovered a rich pocket. With such things actually happening, naturally it followed that every report of a real or rumored strike set the miners crazy. Even those who had good claims always suspected that they might do better elsewhere. It is significant that the miners of that day, like hunters, always had the notion that they had come out to California just one trip too late for the best pickings.

The physical life was very hard, and it is no wonder that the stragglers back from the mines increased in numbers as time went on. It was a true case of survival of the fittest.

Those who remained and became professional miners were the hardiest, most optimistic, and most persistent of the population. The mere physical labor was very severe. Any one not raised as a day laborer who has tried to do a hard day's work in a new garden can understand what pick and shovel digging in the bottoms of gravel and boulder streams can mean. Add to this the fact that every man overworked himself under the pressure of excitement; that he was up to his waist in the cold water from the Sierra snows, with his head exposed at the same time to the tremendous heat of the California sun; throw in for good measure that he generally cooked for himself, and that his food was coarse and badly prepared; and that in his own mind he had no time to attend to the ordinary comforts and decencies of life. It can well be imagined that a man physically unfit must soon succumb. But those who survived seemed to thrive on these hardships.

California camps by their very quaint and whimsical names bear testimony to the overflowing good humor and high spirits of the early miners. No one took anything too seriously, not even his own success or failure.

The very hardness of the life cultivated an ability to snatch joy from the smallest incident. Some of the joking was a little rough, as when some merry jester poured alcohol over a bully's head, touched a match to it, and chased him out of camp yelling, "Man on fire—put him out!"

It is evident that the time was not one for men of very refined or sensitive nature, unless they possessed at bottom the strong iron of character. The ill-balanced were swept away by the current of excitement, and fell readily into dissipation. The pleasures were rude; the life was hearty; vices unknown to their possessors came to the surface. The most significant tendency, and one that had much to do with later social and political life in California, was the leveling effect of just this hard physical labor. The man with a strong back and the most persistent spirit was the superior of the man with education but with weaker muscles. Each man, finding every other man compelled to labor, was on a social equality with the best. The usual superiority of head-workers over hand-workers disappeared. The low-grade man thus felt himself the equal, if not the superior, of any one else on earth, especially as he was generally able to put his hand on what were to him comparative riches. The pride of employment disappeared completely. It was just as honorable to be a cook or a waiter in a restaurant as to dispense the law— where there was any. The period was brief, but while it lasted, it produced a true social democracy. Nor was there any pretense about it. The rudest miner was on a plane of perfect equality with lawyers, merchants, or professional men. Some men dressed in the very height of style, decking themselves out with all the minute care of a dandy; others were not ashamed of, nor did they object to being seen in, ragged garments. No man could be told by his dress.

The great day of days in a mining-camp was Sunday. Some over-enthusiastic fortune-seekers worked the diggings also on that day; but by general consent— uninfluenced, it may be remarked, by religious considerations—the miners repaired to their little town for amusement and relaxation. These little towns were almost all alike. There were usually two or three combined hotels, saloons, and gambling-houses, built of logs, of slabs, of canvas, or of a combination of the three. There was one store that dispensed whiskey as well as dryer goods, and one or two large places of amusement.

On Sunday everything went full blast. The streets were crowded with men; the saloons were well patronized; the gambling games ran all day and late into the night. Wrestling-matches, jumping-matches, other athletic tests, horse-races, lotteries, fortune-telling, singing, anything to get a pinch or two of the dust out of the good-natured miners—all these were going strong.

The American, English, and other continentals mingled freely, with the exception of the French, who kept to themselves. Successful Germans or Hollanders of the more stupid class ran so true to type and were so numerous that they earned the generic name of "Dutch Charley." They have been described as moon-faced, bland, bullet-headed men, with walrus moustaches, and fatuous, placid smiles. Value meant nothing to them. They only knew the difference between having money and having no money. They carried two or three gold watches at the end of long home-made chains of gold nuggets fastened together with links of copper wire. The chains were sometimes looped about their necks, their shoulders, and waists, and even hung down in long festoons. When two or three such Dutch Charleys inhabited one camp, they became deadly rivals in this childlike display, parading slowly up and down the street, casting malevolent glances at each other as they passed.

Shoals of phrenologists, fortune-tellers, and the like, generally drunken old reprobates on their last legs, plied their trades. One artist, giving out under the physical labor of mining, built up a remarkably profitable trade in sketching portraits. Incidentally he had to pay two dollars and a half for every piece of paper! John Kelly, a wandering minstrel with a violin, became celebrated among the camps, and was greeted with enthusiasm wherever he appeared. He probably made more with his fiddle than he could have made with his shovel. The influence of the "forty-two caliber whiskey" was dire, and towards the end of Sunday the sports became pretty rough.

This day was also considered the time for the trial of any cases that had arisen during the week. The miners elected one of their number to act as presiding judge in a "miners' meeting." Justice was dealt out by this man, either on his own authority with the approval of the crowd, or by popular vote. Disputes about property were adjudicated as well as offenses against the criminal code. Thus a body of precedent was slowly built up. A new case before the "alcalde" of Hangtown was often decided on the basis of the procedure at Grub Gulch. The decisions were characterized by direct common sense. It would be most interesting to give adequate examples here, but space forbids. Suffice it to say that a Mexican horse-thief was convicted and severely flogged; and then a collection was taken up for him on the ground that he was on the whole unfortunate. A thief apprehended on a steamboat was punished by a heavy fine for the benefit of a sick man on board.

Sunday evening usually ended by a dance. As women were entirely lacking at first, a proportion of the men was told off to represent the fair sex. At one camp the invariable rule was to consider as ladies those who possessed patches on the seats of their trousers. This was the distinguishing mark. Take it all around, the day was one of noisy, good-humored fun. There was very little sodden drunkenness, and the miners went back to their work on Monday morning with freshened spirits. Probably just this sort of irresponsible ebullition was necessary to balance the hardness of the life.

In each mining-town was at least one Yankee storekeeper. He made the real profits of the mines. His buying ability was considerable; his buying power was often limited by what he could get hold of at the coast and what he could transport to the camps. Often his consignments were quite arbitrary and not at all what he ordered. The story is told of one man who received what, to judge by the smell, he thought was three barrels of spoiled beef. Throwing them out in the back way, he was interested a few days later to find he had acquired a rapidly increasing flock of German scavengers. They seemed to be investigating the barrels and carrying away the spoiled meat. When the barrels were about empty, the storekeeper learned that the supposed meat was in reality sauerkraut!

The outstanding fact about these camps was that they possessed no solidarity. Each man expected to exploit the diggings and then to depart for more congenial climes. He wished to undertake just as little responsibility as he possibly could. With so-called private affairs other than his own he would have nothing to do. The term private affairs was very elastic, stretching often to cover even cool-blooded murder.

When matters arose affecting the whole public welfare in which he himself might possibly become interested, he was roused to the point of administering justice. The punishments meted out were fines, flogging, banishment, and, as a last resort, lynching. Theft was considered a worse offense than killing. As the mines began to fill up with the more desperate characters who arrived in 1850 and 1851, the necessity for government increased. At this time, but after the leveling effect of universal labor had had its full effect, the men of personality, of force and influence, began to come to the front. A fresh aristocracy of ability, of influence, of character was created.

Chapter Nine: The Urban Forty-niner

In popular estimation the interest and romance of the Forty-niners center in gold and mines. To the close student, however, the true significance of their lives is to be found even more in the city of San Francisco.

At first practically everybody came to California under the excitement of the gold rush and with the intention of having at least one try at the mines. But though gold was to be found in unprecedented abundance, the getting of it was at best extremely hard work. Men fell sick both in body and spirit. They became discouraged. Extravagance of hope often resulted, by reaction, in an equal exaggeration of despair. The prices of everything were very high. The cost of medical attendance was almost prohibitory. Men sometimes made large daily sums in the placers; but necessary expenses reduced their net income to small wages.

Ryan gives this account of an interview with a returning miner: "He readily entered into conversation and informed us that he had passed the summer at the mines where the excessive heat during the day, and the dampness of the ground where the gold washing is performed, together with privation and fatigue, had brought on fever and ague which nearly proved fatal to him. He had frequently given an ounce of gold for the visit of a medical man, and on several occasions had paid two and even three ounces for a single dose of medicine. He showed us a pair of shoes, nearly worn out, for which he had paid twenty-four dollars." Later

Ryan says: "Only such men as can endure the hardship and privation incidental to life in the mines are likely to make fortunes by digging for the ore. I am unequal to the task ... I think I could within an hour assemble in this very place from twenty to thirty individuals of my own acquaintance who had all told the same story. They were thoroughly dissatisfied and disgusted with their experiment in the gold country. The truth of the matter is that only traders, speculators, and gamblers make large fortunes."

Only rarely did men of cool enough heads and far enough sight eschew from the very beginning all notion of getting rich quickly in the placers, and deliberately settle down to make their fortunes in other ways.

This conclusion of Ryan's throws, of course, rather too dark a tone over the picture. The "hardy miner" was a reality, and the life in the placers was, to such as he, profitable and pleasant. However, this point of view had its influence in turning back from the mines a very large proportion of those who first went in. Many of them drifted into mercantile pursuits.

Harlan tells us: "During my sojourn in Stockton I mixed freely with the returning and disgusted miners from whom I learned that they were selling their mining implements at ruinously low prices. An idea struck me one day which I immediately acted upon for fear that another might strike in the same place and cause an explosion. The heaven-born idea that had penetrated my cranium was this: start in the mercantile line, purchase the kits and implements of the returning miners at low figures and sell to the greenhorns en route to the mines at California prices."

In this manner innumerable occupations supplying the obvious needs were taken up by many returned miners. A certain proportion drifted to crime or shady devices, but the large majority returned to San Francisco, whence they either went home completely discouraged, or with renewed energy and better-applied ability took hold of the destinies of the new city. Thus another sort of Forty-niner became in his way as significant and strong, as effective and as romantic as his brother, the red-shirted Forty-niner of the diggings.

But in addition to the miners who had made their stakes, who had given up the idea of mining, or who were merely waiting for the winter's rains to be over to go back again to the diggings, an ever increasing immigration was coming to San Francisco with the sole idea of settling in that place. All classes of men were represented. Many of the big mercantile establishments of the East were sending out their agents. Independent merchants sought the rewards of speculation. Gamblers also perceived opportunities for big killings. Professional politicians and cheap lawyers, largely from the Southern States, unfortunately also saw their chance to obtain standing in a new community, having lost all standing in their own. The result of the mixing of these various chemical elements of society was an extraordinary boiling and bubbling.

When Commander Montgomery hoisted the American flag in 1846, the town of Yerba Buena, as San Francisco was called, had a population of about two hundred. Before the discovery of gold it developed under the influence of American enterprise normally and rationally into a prosperous little town with two hotels, a few private dwellings, and two wharves in the process of construction. Merchants had established themselves with connections in the Eastern States, in Great Britain, and South America. Just before the discovery of gold the population had increased to eight hundred and twelve.

The news of the placers practically emptied the town. It would be curious to know exactly how many human souls and chickens remained after Brannan's *California Star* published the authentic news. The commonest necessary activities were utterly neglected, shops were closed and barricaded, merchandise was left rotting on the wharves and the beaches, and the prices of necessities rose to tremendous altitudes. The place looked as a deserted mining-camp does now. The few men left who would work wanted ten or even twenty dollars a day for the commonest labor.

However, the early pioneers were hard-headed citizens. Many of the shopkeepers and merchants, after a short experience of the mines, hurried back to make the inevitable fortune that must come to the middleman in these extraordinary times. Within the first eight weeks of the gold excitement two hundred and fifty thousand dollars in gold dust reached San Francisco, and within: the following eight weeks six hundred thousand dollars more came in. All of this was to purchase supplies at any price for the miners.

This was in the latter days of 1848. In the first part of 1849 the immigrants began to arrive. They had to have places to sleep, things to eat, transportation to the diggings, outfits of various sorts. In the first six months of 1849 ten thousand people piled down upon the little city built to accommodate eight hundred. And the last six months of the year were still more extraordinary, as some thirty thousand more dumped themselves on the chaos of the first immigration. The result can be imagined. The city was mainly of canvas either in the form of tents or of crude canvas and wooden houses. The few substantial buildings stood like rocks in a tossing sea. No attempt, of course, had been made as yet toward public improvements. The streets were ankle-deep in dust or neck-deep in mud. A great smoke of dust hung perpetually over the city, raised by the trade winds of the afternoon. Hundreds of ships lay at anchor in the harbor. They had been deserted by their crews, and, before they could be re-manned, the faster clipper ships, built to control the fluctuating western trade, had displaced them, so that the majority were fated never again to put to sea.

Newcomers landed at first on a flat beach of deep black sand, where they generally left their personal effects for lack of means of transportation. They climbed to a ragged thoroughfare of open sheds and ramshackle buildings, most of them in the course of construction.

Beneath crude shelters of all sorts and in great quantities were goods brought in hastily by eager speculators on the high prices. The four hundred deserted ships lying at anchor in the harbor had dumped down on the new community the most ridiculous assortment of necessities and luxuries, such as calico, silk, rich furniture, mirrors, knock-down houses, cases and cases of tobacco, clothing, statuary, mining-implements, provisions, and the like.

The hotels and lodging houses immediately became very numerous. Though they were in reality only overcrowded bunk-houses, the most enormous prices were charged for beds in them. People lay ten or twenty in a single room—in row after row of cots, in bunks, or on the floor. Between the discomfort of hard beds, fleas, and overcrowding, the entire populace spent most of its time on the street or in the saloons and gambling, houses. As some one has pointed out, this custom added greatly to the apparent population of the place. Gambling was the gaudiest, the best-paying, and the most patronized industry. It occupied the largest structures, and it probably imported and installed the first luxuries.

Of these resorts the El Dorado became the most famous. It occupied at first a large tent but soon found itself forced to move to better quarters. The rents paid for buildings were enormous. Three thousand dollars a month in advance was charged for a single small store made of rough boards. A two-story frame building on Kearny Street near the Plaza paid its owners a hundred and twenty thousand dollars a year rent. The tent containing the El Dorado gambling saloon was rented for forty thousand dollars a year. The prices sky-rocketed still higher. Miners paid as high as two hundred dollars for an ordinary gold rocker, fifteen or twenty dollars for a pick, the same for a shovel, and so forth. A copper coin was considered a curiosity, a half-dollar was the minimum tip for any small service, twenty-five cents was the smallest coin in circulation, and the least price for which anything could be sold. Bread came to fifty cents a loaf. Good boots were a hundred dollars.

Affairs moved very swiftly. A month was the unit of time. Nobody made bargains for more than a month in advance. Interest was charged on money by the month. Indeed, conditions changed so fast that no man pretended to estimate them beyond thirty days ahead, and to do even that was considered rather a gamble.

Real estate joined the parade of advance. Little holes in sand-hills sold for fabulous prices. The sick, destitute, and discouraged were submerged beneath the mounting tide of vigorous optimism that bore on its crest the strong and able members of the community. Every one either was rich or expected soon to be so.

Opportunity awaited every man at every corner. Men who knew how to take advantage of fortune's gifts were assured of immediate high returns. Those with capital were, of course, enabled to take advantage of the opportunities more quickly; but the ingenious mind saw its chances even with nothing to start on.

One man, who landed broke but who possessed two or three dozen old newspapers used as packing, sold them at a dollar and two dollars apiece and so made his start. Another immigrant with a few packages of ordinary tin tacks exchanged them with a man engaged in putting up a canvas house for their exact weight in gold dust.

Harlan tells of walking along the shore of Happy Valley and finding it lined with discarded pickle jars and bottles. Remembering the high price of pickles in San Francisco, he gathered up several hundred of them, bought a barrel of cider vinegar from a newly-arrived vessel, collected a lot of cucumbers, and started a bottling works. Before night, he said, he had cleared over three hundred dollars. With this he made a corner in tobacco pipes by which he realized one hundred and fifty dollars in twenty-four hours.

Mail was distributed soon after the arrival of the mail-steamer. The indigent would often sit up a day or so before the expected arrival of the mail-steamer holding places in line at the post-office. They expected no letters but could sell the advantageous positions for high prices when the mail actually arrived. He was a poor-spirited man indeed who by these and many other equally picturesque means could not raise his gold slug in a reasonable time; and, possessed of fifty dollars, he was an independent citizen. He could increase his capital by interest compounded every day, provided he used his wits; or for a brief span of glory he could live with the best of them.

A story is told of a new-come traveler offering a small boy fifty cents to carry his valise to the hotel. The urchin looked with contempt at the coin, fished out two fifty-cent pieces, handed them to the owner of the valise, saying "Here's a dollar; carry it yourself."

One John A. McGlynn arrived without assets. He appreciated the opportunity for ordinary teaming, and hitching California mules to the only and exceedingly decrepit wagon to be found he started in business. Possessing a monopoly, he charged what he pleased, so that within a short time he had driving for him a New York lawyer, whom he paid a hundred and seventy-five dollars a month. His outfit was magnificent. When somebody joked with him about his legal talent, he replied, "The whole business of a lawyer is to know how to manage mules and asses so as to make them pay." When within a month plenty of wagons were imported, McGlynn had so well established himself and possessed so much character that he became *ex officio* the head of the industry. He was evidently a man of great and solid sense and was looked up to as one of the leading citizens.

Every human necessity was crying out for its ordinary conveniences. There were no streets, there were no hotels, there were no lodging-houses, there were no warehouses, there were no stores, there was no water, there was no fuel. Any one who could improvise anything, even a bare substitute, to satisfy any of these needs, was sure of immense returns. In addition, the populace was so busy—so overwhelmingly busy—with its own affairs that it literally could not spare a moment to govern itself. The professional and daring politicians never had a clearer field. They went to extraordinary lengths in all sorts of grafting, in the sale of public real estate, in every "shenanigan" known to skillful low-grade politicians. Only occasionally did they go too far, as when, in addition to voting themselves salaries of six thousand dollars apiece as aldermen, they coolly voted themselves also gold medals to the value of one hundred and fifty dollars apiece "for public and extra services." Then the determined citizens took an hour off for the council chambers. The medals were cast into the melting-pot.

All writers agree, in their memoirs, that the great impression left on the mind by San Francisco was its extreme busyness. The streets were always crammed full of people running and darting in all directions. It was, indeed, a heterogeneous mixture. Not only did the Caucasian show himself in every extreme of costume, from the most exquisite top-hated dandy to the red-shirted miner, but there were also to be found all the picturesque and unknown races of the earth, the Chinese, the Chileño, the Moor, the Turk, the Mexican, the Spanish, the Islander, not to speak of ordinary foreigners from Russia, England,

France, Belgium, Germany, Italy, and the out-of-the-way corners of Europe.

All these people had tremendous affairs to finish in the least possible time. And every once in a while some individual on horseback would sail down the street at full speed, scattering the crowd left and right. If any one remarked that the marauding individual should be shot, the excuse was always offered, "Oh, well, don't mind him. He's only drunk," as if that excused everything.

Many of the activities of the day also were picturesque. As there were no warehouses in which to store goods, and as the few structures of the sort charged enormous rentals, it was cheaper to auction off immediately all consignments. These auctions were then, and remained for some years, one of the features of the place. The more pretentious dealers kept brass bands to attract the crowd. The returning miners were numerous enough to patronize both these men and the cheap clothing stores, and having bought themselves new outfits, generally cast the old ones into the middle of the street. Water was exceedingly scarce and in general demand, so that laundry work was high. It was the fashion of these gentry to wear their hair and beards long. They sported red shirts, flashy Chinese scarves around their waists, black belts with silver buckles, six-shooters and bowie-knives, and wide floppy hats.

The business of the day over, the evening was open for relaxation. As the hotels and lodging-houses were nothing but kennels, and very crowded kennels, it followed that the entire population gravitated to the saloons and gambling places. Some of these were established on a very extensive scale. They had not yet attained the magnificence of the Fifties, but it is extraordinary to realize that within so few months and at such a great distance from civilization, the early and enterprising managed to take on the trappings of luxury. Even thus early, plate-glass mirrors, expensive furniture, the gaudy, tremendous oil paintings peculiar to such dives, prism chandeliers, and the like, had made their appearance. Later, as will be seen, these gambling dens presented an aspect of barbaric magnificence, unique and peculiar to the time and place. In 1849, however gorgeous the trappings might have appeared to men long deprived of such things, they were of small importance compared with the games themselves. At times the bets were enormous. Soulé tells us that as high as twenty thousand dollars were risked on the turn of one card. The ordinary stake, however, was not so large, from fifty cents to five dollars being about the usual amount.

Even at this the gamblers were well able to pay the high rents. Quick action was the word. The tables were always crowded and bystanders many deep waited to lay their stakes. Within a year or so the gambling resorts assumed rather the nature of club-rooms, frequented by every class, many of whom had no intention of gambling. Men met to talk, read the newspapers, write letters, or perhaps take a turn at the tables. But in 1849 the fever of speculation held every man in its grip.

Again it must be noted how wide an epoch can be spanned by a month or two. The year 1849 was but three hundred and sixty-five days long, and yet in that space the community of San Francisco passed through several distinct phases. It grew visibly like the stalk of a century plant.

Of public improvements there were almost none. The few that were undertaken sprang from absolute necessity. The town got through the summer season fairly well, but, as the winter that year proved to be an unusually rainy time, it soon became evident that something must be done. The streets became bottomless pits of mud. It is stated, as plain and sober fact, that in some of the main thoroughfares teams of mules and horses sank actually out of sight and were suffocated. Foot travel was almost impossible unless across some sort of causeway. Lumber was so expensive that it was impossible to use it for the purpose. Fabulous quantities of goods sent in by speculators loaded the market and would sell so low that it was actually cheaper to use bales of them than to use planks. Thus one muddy stretch was paved with bags of Chilean flour, another with tierces of tobacco, while over still another the wayfarers proceeded on the tops of cook stoves. These sank gradually in the soft soil until the tops were almost level with the mud. Of course one of the first acts of the merry jester was to shy the stove lids off into space.

The footing especially after dark can be imagined. Crossing a street on these things was a perilous traverse watched with great interest by spectators on either side. Often the hardy adventurer, after teetering for some time, would with a descriptive oath sink to his waist in the slimy mud. If the wayfarer was drunk enough, he then proceeded to pelt his tormentors with missiles of the sticky slime. The good humor of the community saved it from absolute despair. Looked at with cold appraising eye, the conditions were decidedly uncomfortable. In addition there was a grimmer side to the picture. Cholera and intermittent fever came, brought in by ships as well as by overland immigrants, and the death-rate rose by leaps and bounds.

The greater the hardships and obstacles, the higher the spirit of the community rose to meet them. In that winter was born the spirit that has animated San Francisco ever since, and that so nobly and cheerfully met the final great trial of the earthquake and fire of 1906.

About this time an undesirable lot of immigrants began to arrive, especially from the penal colonies of New South Wales. The criminals of the latter class soon became known to the populace as "Sydney Ducks." They formed a nucleus for an adventurous, idle, pleasure-loving, dissipated set of young sports, who organized themselves into a loose band very much on the order of the East Side gangs in New York or the "hoodlums" in later San Francisco, with the exception, however, that these young men affected the most meticulous nicety in dress. They perfected in the spring of 1849 an organization called the Regulators, announcing that, as there was no regular police force, they would take it upon themselves to protect the weak against the strong and the newcomer against the bunco man. Every Sunday they paraded the streets with bands and banners. Having no business in the world to occupy them, and holding a position unique in the community, the Regulators soon developed into practically a band of cut-throats and robbers, with the object of relieving those too weak to bear alone the weight of wealth.

The Regulators, or Hounds, as they soon came to be called, had the great wisdom to avoid the belligerent and resourceful pioneer. They issued from their headquarters, a large tent near the Plaza, every night. Armed with clubs and pistols, they descended upon the settlements of harmless foreigners living near the outskirts, relieved them of what gold dust they possessed, beat them up by way of warning, and returned to headquarters with the consciousness of a duty well done. The victims found it of little use to appeal to the *alcalde,* for with the best disposition in the world the latter could do nothing without an adequate police force. The ordinary citizen, much too interested in his own affairs, merely took precautions to preserve his own skin, avoided dark and unfrequented alleyways, barricaded his doors and windows, and took the rest out in contemptuous cursing.

Encouraged by this indifference, the Hounds naturally grew bolder and bolder. They considered they had terrorized the rest of the community, and they began to put on airs and swagger in the usual manner of bullies everywhere. On Sunday afternoon of July 15, they made a raid on some California ranchos across the bay, ostensibly as a picnic expedition, returning triumphant and very drunk. For the rest of the afternoon with streaming banners they paraded the streets, discharging firearms and generally shooting up the town. At dark they descended upon the Chilean quarters, tore down the tents, robbed the Chileans, beat many of the men to insensibility, ousted the women, killed a number who had not already fled, and returned to town only the following morning.

This proved to be the last straw. The busy citizens dropped their own affairs for a day and got together in a mass meeting at the Plaza. All work was suspended and all business houses were closed. Probably all the inhabitants in the city with the exception of the Hounds had gathered together. Our old friend, Sam Brannan, possessing the gift of a fiery spirit and an arousing tongue, addressed the meeting. A sum of money was raised for the despoiled foreigners. An organization was effected, and armed *posses* were sent out to arrest the ringleaders. They had little difficulty. Many left town for foreign parts or for the mines, where they met an end easily predicted. Others were condemned to various punishments. The Hounds were thoroughly broken up in an astonishingly brief time.

The real significance of their great career is that they called to the attention of the better class of citizens the necessity for at least a sketchy form of government and a framework of law. Such matters as city revenue were brought up for practically the first time.

Gambling-houses were made to pay a license. Real estate, auction sales, and other licenses were also taxed. One of the ships in the harbor was drawn up on shore and was converted into a jail. A district-attorney was elected, with an associate. The whole municipal structure was still about as rudimentary as the streets into which had been thrown armfuls of brush in a rather hopeless attempt to furnish an artificial bottom.

It was a beginning, however, and men had at last turned their eyes even momentarily from their private affairs to consider the welfare of this unique society which was in the making.

Chapter Ten: Ordeal by Fire

San Francisco in the early years must be considered, aside from the interest of its picturesqueness and aside from its astonishing growth, as a crucible of character. Men had thrown off all moral responsibility.

Gambling, for example, was a respectable amusement. People in every class of life frequented the gambling saloons openly and without thought of apology. Men were leading a hard and vigorous life; the reactions were quick; and diversions were eagerly seized. Decent women were absolutely lacking, and the women of the streets had as usual followed the army of invasion. It was not considered at all out of the ordinary to frequent their company in public, and men walked with them by day to the scandal of nobody. There was neither law nor restraint. Most men were drunk with sudden wealth. The battle was, as ever, to the strong.

There was every inducement to indulge the personal side of life. As a consequence, many formed habits they could not break, spent all of their money on women and drink and gambling, ruined themselves in pocket-book and in health, returned home broken, remained sodden and hopeless tramps, or joined the criminal class.

Thousands died of cholera or pneumonia; hundreds committed suicide; but those who came through formed the basis of a race remarkable today for its strength, resourcefulness, and optimism. Characters solid at bottom soon come to the inevitable reaction. They were the forefathers of a race of people which is certainly different from the inhabitants of any other portion of the country.

The first public test came with the earliest of the big fires that, within the short space of eighteen months, six times burned San Francisco to the ground. This fire occurred on December 4, 1849. It was customary in the saloons to give negroes a free drink and tell them not to come again. One did come again to Dennison's; he was flogged, and knocked over a lamp. Thus there started a conflagration that consumed over a million dollars' worth of property. The valuable part of the property, it must be confessed, was in the form of goods, is the light canvas and wooden shacks were of little worth. Possibly the fire consumed enough germs and germ-breeding dirt to pay partially for itself. Before the ashes had cooled, the enterprising real estate owners were back re-erecting the destroyed structures.

This first fire was soon followed by others, each intrinsically severe.

The people were splendid in enterprise and spirit of recovery; but they soon realized that not only must the buildings be made of more substantial material, but also that fire-fighting apparatus must be bought.

In June, 1850, four hundred houses were destroyed; in May, 1851, a thousand were burned at a loss of two million and a half; in June, 1851, the town was razed to the water's edge. In many places the wharves were even disconnected from the shore. Everywhere deep holes were burned in them, and some people fell through at night and were drowned. In this fire a certain firm, Dewitt and Harrison, saved their warehouse by knocking in barrels of vinegar and covering their building with blankets soaked in that liquid. Water was unobtainable. It was reported that they thus used eighty thousand gallons of vinegar, but saved their warehouse.

The loss now had amounted to something like twelve million dollars for the large fires. It became more evident that something must be done.

From the exigencies of the situation were developed the volunteer companies, which later became powerful political, as well as fire-fighting, organizations. There were many of these.

In the old Volunteer Department there were fourteen engines, three hook-and-ladder companies, and a number of hose companies. Each possessed its own house, which was in the nature of a club-house, well supplied with reading and drinking matter. The members of each company were strongly partisan. They were ordinarily drawn from men of similar tastes and position in life. Gradually they came to stand also for similar political interests, and thus grew to be, like New York's Tammany Hall, instruments of the politically ambitious.

On an alarm of fire the members at any time of the day and night ceased their occupation or leaped from their beds to run to the engine-house.

Thence the hand-engines were dragged through the streets at a terrific rate of speed by hundreds of yelling men at the end of the ropes. The first engine at a fire obtained the place of honor; therefore every alarm was the signal for a breakneck race. Arrived at the scene of fire, the water-box of one engine was connected by hose with the reservoir of the next, and so water was relayed from engine to engine until it was thrown on the flames. The motive power of the pump was supplied by the crew of each engine. The men on either side manipulated the pump by jerking the hand-rails up and down. Putting out the fire soon became a secondary matter. The main object of each company was to "wash" its rival; that is, to pump water into the water box of the engine ahead faster than the latter could pump it out, thus overflowing and eternally disgracing its crew. The foremen walked back and forth between the rails, as if on quarter-decks, exhorting their men. Relays in uniform stood ready on either side to take the place of those who were exhausted. As the race became closer, the foremen would get more excited, begging their crews to increase the speed of the stroke, beating their speaking trumpets into shapeless and battered relics.

In the meantime the hook-and-ladder companies were plying their glorious and destructive trade. A couple of firemen would mount a ladder to the eaves of the house to be attacked, taking with them a heavy hook at the end of a long pole or rope. With their axes they cut a small hole in the eaves, hooked on this apparatus, and descended. At once as many firemen and volunteers as could get hold of the pole and the rope began to pull.

The timbers would crack, break; the whole side of the house would come out with a grand satisfying smash. In this way the fire within was laid open to the attack of the hose-men. This sort of work naturally did little toward saving the building immediately affected, but it was intended to confine or check the fire within the area already burning.

The occasion was a grand jubilation for every boy in the town—which means every male of any age. The roar of the flames, the hissing of the steam, the crash of the timber, the shrieks of the foremen, the yells of applause or of sarcastic comment from the crowd, and the thud of the numerous pumps made a glorious row. Everybody, except the owners of the buildings, was hugely delighted, and when the fire was all over it was customary for the unfortunate owner further to increase the amount of his loss by dealing out liquid refreshments to everybody concerned.

On parade days each company turned out with its machine brought to a high state of polish by varnish, and with the members resplendent in uniform, carrying pole-axes and banners. If the rivalries at the fire could only be ended in a general free fight, everybody was the better satisfied.

Thus by the end of the first period of its growth three necessities had compelled the careless new city to take thought of itself and of public convenience. The mud had forced the cleaning and afterwards the planking of the principal roads; the Hounds had compelled the adoption of at least a semblance of government; and the repeated fires had made necessary the semiofficial organization of the fire department.

By the end of 1850 we find that a considerable amount of actual progress has been made. This came not in the least from any sense of civic pride but from the pressure of stern necessity. The new city now had eleven wharves, for example, up to seventeen hundred feet in length. It had done no little grading of its sand-hills. The quagmire of its streets had been filled and in some places planked. Sewers had been installed. Flimsy buildings were being replaced by substantial structures, for which the stones in some instances were imported from China.

Yet it must be repeated that at this time little or no progress sprang from civic pride. Each man was for himself. But, unlike the native Californian, he possessed wants and desires which had to be satisfied, and to that end he was forced, at least in essentials, to accept responsibility and to combine with his neighbors.

The machinery of this early civic life was very crude. Even the fire department, which was by far the most efficient, was, as has been indicated, more occupied with politics, rivalry, and fun, than with its proper function. The plank roads were good as long as they remained unworn, but they soon showed many holes, large and small, jagged, splintered, ugly holes going down into the depths of the mud. Many of these had been mended by private philanthropists; many more had been labeled with facetious signboards. There were rough sketches of accidents taken from life, and various legends such as "Head of Navigation," "No bottom," "Horse and dray lost here," "Take sounding," "Storage room, inquire below," "Good fishing for teal," and the like.

As for the government, the less said about that the better. Responsibility was still in embryo; but politics and the law, as an irritant, were highly esteemed. The elections of the times were a farce and a holiday; nobody knew whom he was voting for nor what he was shouting for, but he voted as often and shouted as loud as he could. Every American citizen was entitled to a vote, and every one, no matter from what part of the world he came, claimed to be an American citizen and defied any one to prove the contrary. Proof consisted of club, sling-shot, bowie, and pistol. A grand free fight was a refreshment to the soul. After "a pleasant time by all was had," the populace settled down and forgot all about the officers whom it had elected. The latter went their own sweet way, unless admonished by spasmodic mass-meetings that some particularly unscrupulous raid on the treasury was noted and resented. Most of the revenue was made by the sale of city lots. Scrip was issued in payment of debt. This bore interest sometimes at the rate of six or eight per cent a month.

In the meantime, the rest of the crowd went about its own affairs. Then, as now, the American citizen is willing to pay a very high price in dishonesty to be left free for his own pressing affairs. That does not mean that he is himself either dishonest or indifferent. When the price suddenly becomes too high, either because of the increase in dishonesty or the decrease in value of his own time, he suddenly refuses to pay.

This happened not infrequently in the early days of California.

Chapter Eleven: The Vigilantes of '51

In 1851 the price for one commodity became too high. That commodity was lawlessness.

In two years the population of the city had vastly increased, until it now numbered over thirty thousand inhabitants. At an equal or greater pace the criminal and lawless elements had also increased. The confessedly criminal immigrants were paroled convicts from Sydney and other criminal colonies. These practiced men were augmented by the weak and desperate from other countries. Mexico, especially, was strongly represented. At first few in numbers and poverty-stricken in resources, these men acted merely as footpads, highwaymen, and cheap crooks. As time went on, however, they gradually became more wealthy and powerful, until they had established a sort of caste. They had not the social importance of many of the "higher-ups" of 1856, but they were crude, powerful, and in many cases wealthy. They were ably seconded by a class of lawyers which then, and for some years later, infested the courts of California. These men had made little success at law, or perhaps had been driven forth from their native haunts because of evil practices.

They played the game of law exactly as the cheap criminal lawyer does today, but with the added advantage that their activities were controlled neither by a proper public sentiment nor by the usual discipline of better colleagues. Unhappily we are not yet far enough removed from just this perversion to need further explanation of the method. Indictments were fought for the reason that the murderer's name was spelled wrong in one letter; because, while the accusation stated that the murderer killed his victim with a pistol, it did not say that it was by the discharge of said pistol; and so on. But patience could not endure forever. The decent element of the community was forced at last to beat the rascals. Its apparent indifference had been only preoccupation.

The immediate cause was the cynical and open criminal activity of an Englishman named James Stuart. This man was a degenerate criminal of the worst type, who came into a temporary glory through what he considered the happy circumstances of the time. Arrested for one of his crimes, he seemed to anticipate the usual very good prospects of escaping all penalties. There had been dozens of exactly similar incidents, but this one proved to be the spark to ignite a long gathering pile of kindling. One hundred and eighty-four of the wealthiest and most prominent men of the city formed themselves into a secret Committee of Vigilance. As is usual when anything of importance is to be done, the busiest men of the community were summoned and put to work. Strangely enough, the first trial under this Committee of Vigilance resulted also in a divided jury. The mob of eight thousand or more people who had gathered to see justice done by others than the appointed court finally though grumblingly acquiesced. The prisoners were turned over to the regular authorities, and were eventually convicted and sentenced.

So far from being warned by this popular demonstration, the criminal offenders grew bolder than ever. The second great fire, in May, 1851, was commonly believed to be the work of incendiaries. Patience ceased to be a virtue. The time for resolute repression of crime had arrived.

In June the Vigilance Committee was formally organized. Our old and picturesque friend Sam Brannan was deeply concerned. In matters of initiative for the public good, especially where a limelight was concealed in the wing, Brannan was an able and efficient citizen.

Headquarters were chosen and a formal organization was perfected. The Monumental Fire Engine Company bell was to be tolled as a summons for the Committee to meet. Even before the first meeting had adjourned, this signal was given. A certain John Jenkins had robbed a safe and was caught after a long and spectacular pursuit. Jenkins was an Australian convict and was known to numerous people as an old offender in many ways. He was therefore typical of the exact thing the Vigilance Committee had been formed to prevent. By eleven o'clock the trial, which was conducted with due decorum and formality, was over. Jenkins was adjudged guilty. There was no disorder either before or after Jenkins's trial. Throughout the trial and subsequent proceedings Jenkins's manner was unafraid and arrogant.

He fully expected not only that the nerve of the Committee would give out, but that at any moment he would be rescued. It must be remembered that the sixty or seventy men in charge were known as peaceful unwarlike merchants, and that against them were arrayed all the belligerent swashbucklers of the town. While the trial was going on, the Committee was informed by its officers outside that already the roughest characters throughout the city had been told of the organization, and were gathering for rescue. The prisoner insulted his captors, still unconvinced that they meant business; then he demanded a clergyman, who prayed for three-quarters of an hour straight, until Mr. Ryckman, hearing of the gathering for rescue, no longer contained himself. Said he: "Mr. Minister, you have now prayed three-quarters of an hour. I want you to bring this prayer business to a halt. I am going to hang this man in fifteen minutes."

The Committee itself was by no means sure at all times. Bancroft tells us that "one time during the proceedings there appeared some faltering on the part of the judges, or rather a hesitancy to take the lead in assuming responsibility and braving what might be subsequent odium. It was one thing for a half-drunken rabble to take the life of a fellow man, but quite another thing for staid church-going men of business to do it. Then it was that William A. Howard, after watching the proceedings for a few moments, rose, and laying his revolver on the table looked over the assembly. Then with a slow enunciation he said, 'Gentlemen, as I understand it, we are going to hang somebody.' There was no more halting."

While these things were going on, Sam Brannan was sent out to communicate to the immense crowd the Committee's decision. He was instructed by Ryckman, "Sam, you go out and harangue the crowd while we make ready to move." Brannan was an ideal man for just such a purpose. He was of an engaging personality, of coarse fiber, possessed of a keen sense of humor, a complete knowledge of crowd psychology, and a command of ribald invective that carried far. He spoke for some time, and at the conclusion boldly asked the crowd whether or not the Committee's action met with its approval. The response was naturally very much mixed, but like a true politician Sam took the result he wanted. They found the lovers of order had already procured for them two ropes, and had gathered into some sort of coherence. The procession marched to the Plaza where Jenkins was duly hanged. The lawless element gathered at the street corners, and at least one abortive attempt at rescue was started.

But promptness of action combined with the uncertainty of the situation carried the Committee successfully through. The coroner's jury next day brought in a verdict that the deceased "came to his death on the part of an association styling themselves a Committee on Vigilance, of whom the following members are implicated." And then followed nine names. The Committee immediately countered by publishing its roster of one hundred and eighty names in full.

The organization that was immediately perfected was complete and interesting. This was an association that was banded together and close-knit, and not merely a loose body of citizens. It had headquarters, company organizations, police, equipment, laws of its own, and a regular routine for handling the cases brought before it. Its police force was large and active. Had the Vigilance movement in California begun and ended with the Committee of 1851, it would be not only necessary but most interesting to follow its activities in detail.

But, as it was only the forerunner and trail-blazer for the greater activities of 1856, we must save our space and attention for the latter.

Suffice it to say that, with only nominal interference from the law, the first Committee hanged four people and banished a great many more for the good of their country. Fifty executions in the ordinary way would have had little effect on the excited populace of the time; but in the peculiar circumstances these four deaths accomplished a moral regeneration. This revival of public conscience could not last long, to be sure, but the worst criminals were, at least for the time being, cowed.

Spasmodic efforts toward coherence were made by the criminals, but these attempts all proved abortive. Inflammatory circulars and newspaper articles, small gatherings, hidden threats, were all freely indulged in.

At one time a rescue of two prisoners was accomplished, but the Monumental bell called together a determined band of men who had no great difficulty in reclaiming their own. The Governor of the State, secretly in sympathy with the purposes of the Committee, was satisfied to issue a formal proclamation.

It must be repeated that, were it not for the later larger movement of 1856, this Vigilance Committee would merit more extended notice. It gave a lead, however, and a framework on which the Vigilance Committee of 1856 was built. It proved that the better citizens, if aroused, could take matters into their own hands. But the opposing forces of 1851 were very different from those of five years later. And the transition from the criminal of 1851 to the criminal of 1856 is the history of San Francisco between those two dates.

Chapter Twelve: San Francisco in Transition

By the mid-fifties San Francisco had attained the dimensions of a city. Among other changes of public interest within the brief space of two or three years were a hospital, a library, a cemetery, several churches, public markets, bathing establishments, public schools, two race-courses, twelve wharves, five hundred and thirty-seven saloons, and about eight thousand women of several classes. The population was now about fifty thousand. The city was now of a fairly substantial character, at least in the down-town districts. There were many structures of brick and stone. In many directions the sand-hills had been conveniently graded down by means of a power shovel called the Steam Paddy in contradistinction to the hand Paddy, or Irishman with a shovel. The streets were driven straight ahead regardless of contours.

It is related that often the inhabitants of houses perched on the sides of the sand-hills would have to scramble to safety as their dwellings rolled down the bank, undermined by some grading operation below. A water system had been established, the nucleus of the present Spring Valley Company. The streets had nearly all been planked, and private enterprise had carried the plank toll-road even to the Mission district.

The fire department had been brought to a high state of perfection. The shallow waters of the bay were being filled up by the rubbish from the town and by the debris from the operations of the Steam Paddies. New streets were formed on piles extended out into the bay. Houses were erected, also on piles and on either side of these marine thoroughfares. Gradually the rubbish filled the skeleton framework.

Occasionally old ships, caught by this seaward invasion, were built around, and so became integral parts of the city itself.

The same insistent demand that led to increasing the speed of the vessels, together with the fact that it cost any ship from one hundred to two hundred dollars a day to lie at any of the wharves, developed an extreme efficiency in loading and unloading cargoes. Hittell says that probably in no port of the world could a ship be emptied as quickly as at San Francisco. For the first and last time in the history of the world the profession of stevedore became a distinguished one.

In addition to the overseas trade, there were now many ships, driven by sail or steam, plying the local routes. Some of the river steamboats had actually been brought around the Horn. Their free-board had been raised by planking-in the lower deck, and thus these frail vessels had sailed their long and stormy voyage—truly a notable feat.

It did not pay to hold goods very long. Eastern shippers seemed, by a curious unanimity, to send out many consignments of the same scarcity. The result was that the high prices of today would be utterly destroyed by an oversupply of tomorrow. It was thus to the great advantage of every merchant to meet his ship promptly, and to gain knowledge as soon as possible of the cargo of the incoming vessels. For this purpose signal stations were established, rowboat patrols were organized, and many other ingenious schemes was applied to the secret service of the mercantile business. Both in order to save storage and to avoid the possibility of loss from new shipments coming in, the goods were auctioned off as soon as they were landed.

These auctions were most elaborate institutions involving brass bands, comfortable chairs, eloquent "spielers," and all the rest. They were a feature of the street life, which in turn had an interest all its own.

The planking threw back a hollow reverberating sound from the various vehicles. There seemed to be no rules of the road. Omnibuses careered along, every window rattling loudly; drays creaked and strained; non-descript delivery wagons tried to outrattle the omnibuses; horsemen picked their way amid the melee. The din was described as something extraordinary—hoofs drumming, wheels rumbling, oaths and shouts, and from the sidewalk the blare and bray of brass bands before the various auction shops. Newsboys and bootblacks darted in all directions. Cigar boys, a peculiar product of the time, added to the hubbub. Boot-blacking stands of the most elaborate description were kept by French and Italians. The town was full of characters who delighted in their own eccentricities, and who were always on public view. One individual possessed a remarkably intelligent pony who every morning, without guidance from his master, patronized one of the shoe-blacking stands to get his front hoofs polished. He presented each one in turn to the foot-rest, and stood like a statue until the job was done.

Some of the numberless saloons already showed signs of real magnificence. Mahogany bars with brass rails, huge mirrors in gilt frames, pyramids of delicate crystal, rich hangings, oil paintings of doubtful merit but indisputable interest, heavy chandeliers of glass prisms, the most elaborate of free lunches, skillful barkeepers who mixed drinks at arm's length, were common to all the better places.

These things would not be so remarkable in large cities at the present time, but in the early Fifties, only three years after the tent stage, and thousands of miles from the nearest civilization, the enterprise that was displayed seemed remarkable. The question of expense did not stop these early worthies. Of one saloonkeeper it is related that, desiring a punch bowl and finding that the only vessel of the sort was a soup-tureen belonging to a large and expensive dinner set, he bought the whole set for the sake of the soup-tureen. Some of the more pretentious places boasted of special attractions: thus one supported its ceiling on crystal pillars; another had dashing young women to serve the drinks, though the mixing was done by men as usual; a third possessed a large musical-box capable of playing several very noisy tunes; a fourth had imported a marvelous piece of mechanism run by clockwork which exhibited the sea in motion, a ship tossing on the waves, on shore a windmill in action, a train of cars passing over a bridge, a deer chased by hounds, and the like.

But these bar-rooms were a totally different institution from the gambling resorts. Although gambling was not now considered the entirely worthy occupation of a few years previous, and although some of the better citizens, while frequenting the gambling halls, still preferred to do their own playing in semi-private, the picturesqueness and glory of these places had not yet been dimmed by any general popular disapproval. The gambling halls were not only places to risk one's fortune, but they were also a sort of evening club. They usually supported a raised stage with footlights, a negro minstrel troop, or a singer or so. On one side elaborate bars of rosewood or mahogany ran the entire length, backed by big mirrors of French plate. The whole of the very large main floor was heavily carpeted. Down the center generally ran two rows of gambling tables offering various games such as faro, keeno, roulette, poker, and the dice games. Beyond these tables, on the opposite side of the room from the bar, were the lounging quarters, with small tables, large easy-chairs, settees, and fireplaces. Decoration was of the most ornate. The ceilings and walls were generally white with a great deal of gilt. All classes of people frequented these places and were welcomed there. Some were dressed in the height of fashion, and some wore the roughest sort of miners' clothes—floppy old slouch hats, flannel shirts, boots to which the dried mud was clinging or from which it fell to the rich carpet. All were considered on an equal plane.

The professional gamblers came to represent a type of their own,—weary, indifferent, pale, cool men, who had not only to keep track of the game and the bets, but also to assure control over the crowd about them. Often in these places immense sums were lost or won; often in these places occurred crimes of shooting and stabbing; but also into these places came many men who rarely drank or gambled at all. They assembled to enjoy each other's company, the brightness, the music, and the sociable warmth.

On Sunday the populace generally did one of two things: either it sallied out in small groups into the surrounding country on picnics or celebrations at some of the numerous road-houses; or it swarmed out the plank toll-road to the Mission. To the newcomer the latter must have been much the more interesting. There he saw a congress of all the nations of the earth: French, Germans, Italians, Russians, Dutchmen, British, Turks, Arabs, Negroes, Chinese, Kanakas, Indians, the gorgeous members of the Spanish races, and all sorts of queer people to whom no habitat could be assigned. Most extraordinary perhaps were the men from the gold mines of the Sierras. The miners had by now distinctly segregated themselves from the rest of the population. They led a hardier, more laborious life and were proud of the fact. They attempted generally to differentiate themselves in appearance from all the rest of the human race, and it must be confessed that they succeeded. The miners were mostly young and wore their hair long, their beards rough; they walked with a wide swagger; their clothes were exaggeratedly coarse, but they ornamented themselves with bright silk handkerchiefs, feathers, flowers, with squirrel or buck tails in their hats, with long heavy chains of nuggets, with glittering and prominently displayed pistols, revolvers, stilettos, knives, and dirks. Some even plaited their beards in three tails, or tied their long hair under their chins; but no matter how bizarre they made themselves, nobody on the streets of *blasé* San Francisco paid the slightest attention to them. The Mission, which they, together with the crowd, frequented, was a primitive Coney Island. Bear pits, cockfights, theatrical attractions, side-shows, innumerable hotels and small restaurants, saloons, races, hammer-striking, throwing balls at negroes' heads, and a hundred other attractions kept the crowds busy and generally good-natured. If a fight arose, "it was," as the Irishman says, "considered a private fight," and nobody else could get in it.

Such things were considered matters for the individuals themselves to settle.

The great feature of the time was its extravagance. It did not matter whether a man was a public servant, a private and respected citizen, or from one of the semi-public professions that cater to men's greed and dissipation, he acted as though the ground beneath his feet were solid gold. The most extravagant public works were undertaken without thought and without plan. The respectable women vied in the magnificence and ostentation of their costumes with the women of the lower world. Theatrical attractions at high prices were patronized abundantly. Balls of great magnificence were given almost every night. Private carriages of really excellent appointment were numerous along the disreputable planked roads or the sandy streets strewn with cans and garbage.

The feverish life of the times reflected itself domestically. No live red-blooded man could be expected to spend his evenings reading a book quietly at home while all the magnificent, splendid, seething life of down-town was roaring in his ears. All his friends would be out; all the news of the day passed around; all the excitements of the evening offered themselves. It was too much to expect of human nature. The consequence was that a great many young wives were left alone, with the ultimate result of numerous separations and divorces. The moral nucleus of really respectable society—and there was a noticeable one even at that time—was overshadowed and swamped for the moment. Such a social life as this sounds decidedly immoral but it was really unmoral, with the bright, eager, attractive immorality of the vigorous child. In fact, in that society, as some one has expressed it, everything was condoned except meanness.

It was the era of the grandiose. Even conversation reflected this characteristic. The myriad bootblacks had grand outfits and stands. The captain of a ship offered ten dollars to a negro to act as his cook. The negro replied, "If you will walk up to my restaurant, I'll set you to work at twenty-five dollars immediately." From men in such humble stations up to the very highest and most respected citizens the spirit of gambling, of taking chances, was also in the air.

As has been pointed out, a large proportion of the city's wealth was raised not from taxation but from the sale of its property. Under the heedless extravagance of the first government the municipal debt rose to over one million dollars. Since interest charged on this was thirty-six per cent annually, it can be seen that the financial situation was rather hopeless. As the city was even then often very short of funds, it paid for its work and its improvements in certificates of indebtedness, usually called "scrip." Naturally this scrip was held below par—a condition that caused all contractors and supply merchants to charge two or three hundred per cent over the normal prices for their work and commodities in order to keep even. And this practice, completing the vicious circle, increased the debt. An attempt was made to fund the city debt by handing in the scrip in exchange for a ten per cent obligation.

This method gave promise of success; but a number of holders of scrip refused to surrender it, and brought suit to enforce payment. One of these, a physician named Peter Smith, was owed a considerable sum for the care of indigent sick. He obtained a judgment against the city, levied on some of its property, and proceeded to sell. The city commissioners warned the public that titles under the Smith claim were not legal, and proceeded to sell the property on their own account. The speculators bought claims under Peter Smith amounting to over two millions of dollars at merely nominal rates. For example, one parcel of city lots sold at less than ten cents per lot. The prices were so absurd that these sales were treated as a joke. The joke came in on the other side, however, when the officials proceeded to ratify these sales. The public then woke up to the fact that it had been fleeced. Enormous prices were paid for unsuitable property, ostensibly for the uses of the city. After the money had passed, these properties were often declared unsuitable and resold at reduced prices to people already determined upon by the ring.

Nevertheless commercially things went well for a time. The needs of hundreds of thousands of newcomers, in a country where the manufactures were practically nothing, were enormous. It is related that at first laundry was sent as far as the Hawaiian Islands. Every single commodity of civilized life, such as we understand it, had to be imported. As there was then no remote semblance of combination, either in restraint of or in encouragement of trade, it followed that the market must fluctuate wildly. The local agents of eastern firms were often embarrassed and overwhelmed by the ill-timed consignments of goods. One Boston firm was alleged to have sent out a whole shipload of women's bonnets—to a community where a woman was one of the rarest sights to be found! Not many shipments were as silly as this, but the fact remains that a rumor of a shortage in any commodity would often be followed by rush orders on clipper ships laden to the guards with that same article.

As a consequence the bottom fell out of the market completely, and the unfortunate consignee found himself forced to auction off the goods much below cost.

During the year 1854, the tide of prosperity began to ebb. A dry season caused a cessation of mining in many parts of the mountains. Of course it can be well understood that the immense prosperity of the city, the prosperity that allowed it to recover from severe financial disease, had its spring in the placer mines. A constant stream of fresh gold was needed to shore up the tottering commercial structure. With the miners out of the diggings, matters changed. The red-shirted digger of gold had little idea of the value of money. Many of them knew only the difference between having money and having none. They had to have credit, which they promptly wasted. Extending credit to the miners made it necessary that credit should also be extended to the sellers, and so on back.

Meanwhile the eastern shippers continued to pour goods into the flooded market. An auction brought such cheap prices that they proved a temptation even to an overstocked public. The gold to pay for purchases went east, draining the country of bullion.

One or two of the supposedly respectable and polished citizens such as Talbot Green and "honest Harry Meiggs" fell by the wayside. The confidence of the new community began to be shaken.

In 1854 came the crisis. Three hundred out of about a thousand business houses shut down. Seventy-seven filed petitions in insolvency with liabilities for many millions of dollars.

In 1855 one hundred and ninety-seven additional firms and several banking houses went under.

There were two immediate results of this state of affairs. In the first place, every citizen became more intensely interested and occupied with his own personal business than ever before; he had less time to devote to the real causes of trouble, that is the public instability; and he grew rather more selfish and suspicious of his neighbor than ever before. The second result was to attract the dregs of society. The pickings incident to demoralized conditions looked rich to these men. Professional politicians, shyster lawyers, political gangsters, flocked to the spoil.

In 1851 the lawlessness of mere physical violence had come to a head. By 1855 and 1856 there was added to a recrudescence of this disorder a lawlessness of graft, of corruption, both political and financial, and the overbearing arrogance of a self-made aristocracy.

These conditions combined to bring about a second crisis in the precarious life of this new society.

Chapter Thirteen: The Storm Gathers

The foundation of trouble in California at this time was formal legalism. Legality was made a fetish. The law was a game played by lawyers and not an attempt to get justice done. The whole of public prosecution was in the hands of one man, generally poorly paid, with equally underpaid assistants, while the defense was conducted by the ablest and most enthusiastic men procurable. It followed that convictions were very few. To lose a criminal case was considered even mildly disgraceful. It was a point of professional pride for the lawyer to get his client free, without reference to the circumstances of the time or the guilt of the accused. To fail was a mark of extreme stupidity, for the game was considered an easy and fascinating one. The whole battery of technical delays was at the command of the defendant.

If a man had neither the time nor the energy for the finesse that made the interest of the game, he could always procure interminable delays during which witnesses could be scattered or else wearied to the point of non-appearance. Changes of venue to courts either prejudiced or known to be favorable to the technical interpretation of the law were very easily procured. Even of shadier expedients, such as packing juries, there was no end.

With these shadier expedients, however, your high-minded lawyer, moving in the best society, well dressed, proud, looked up to, and today possessing descendants who gaze back upon their pioneer ancestors with pride, had little directly to do. He called in as counsel other lawyers, not so high-minded, so honorable, so highly placed. These little lawyers, shoulder-strikers, bribe-givers and takers, were held in good-humored contempt by the legal lights who employed them. The actual dishonesty was diluted through so many agents that it seemed an almost pure stream of lofty integrity. Ordinary jury-packing was an easy art.

Of course the sheriff's office must connive at naming the talesmen; therefore it was necessary to elect the sheriff; consequently all the lawyers were in politics. Of course neither the lawyer nor the sheriff himself ever knew of any individual transaction! A sum of money was handed by the leading counsel to his next in command and charged off as "expense." This fund emerged considerably diminished in the sheriff's office as "perquisites."

Such were the conditions in the realm of criminal law, the realm where the processes became so standardized that between 1849 and 1856 over one thousand murders had been committed and only one legal conviction had been secured! Dueling was a recognized institution, and a skillful shot could always "get" his enemy in this formal manner; but if time or skill lacked, it was still perfectly safe to shoot him down in a street brawl—provided one had money enough to employ talent for defense.

But, once in politics, the law could not stop at the sheriff's office. It rubbed shoulders with big contracts and big financial operations of all sorts. The city was being built within a few years out of nothing by a busy, careless, and shifting population. Money was still easy, people could and did pay high taxes without a thought, for they would rather pay well to be let alone than be bothered with public affairs. Like hyenas to a kill, the public contractors gathered. Immense public works were undertaken at enormous prices. To get their deals through legally it was, of course, necessary that officials, councilmen, engineers, and others should be sympathetic. So, naturally, the big operators as well as the big lawyers had to go into politics. Legal efficiency coupled with the inefficiency of the bench, legal corruption, and the arrogance of personal favor, dissolved naturally into political corruption.

The elections of those days would have been a joke had they been not so tragically significant. They came to be a sheer farce. The polls were guarded by bullies who did not hesitate at command to manhandle any decent citizen indicated by the local leaders. Such men were openly hired for the purposes of intimidation. Votes could be bought in the open market. "Floaters" were shamelessly imported into districts that might prove doubtful; and, if things looked close, the election inspectors and the judges could be relied on to make things come out all right in the final count.

One of the exhibits later shown in the Vigilante days of 1856 was an ingenious ballot box by which the goats could be segregated from the sheep as the ballots were cast. You may be sure that the sheep were the only ones counted. Election day was one of continuous whiskey drinking and brawling so that decent citizens were forced to remain within doors. The returns from the different wards were announced as fast as the votes were counted. It was therefore the custom to hold open certain wards until the votes of all the others were known. Then whatever tickets were lacking to secure the proper election were counted from the packed ballot box in the sure ward. In this manner five hundred votes were once returned from Crystal Springs precinct where there dwelt not over thirty voters. If some busybody made enough of a row to get the merry tyrants into court, there were always plenty of lawyers who could play the ultra-technical so well that the accused were not only released but were returned as legally elected as well.

With the proper officials in charge of the executive end of the government and with a trained crew of lawyers making their own rules as they went along, almost any crime of violence, corruption, theft, or the higher grades of finance could be committed with absolute impunity. The state of the public mind became for a while apathetic. After numberless attempts to obtain justice, the public fell back with a shrug of the shoulders. The men of better feeling found themselves helpless. As each man's safety and ability to resent insult depended on his trigger finger, the newspapers of that time made interesting but scurrilous and scandalous reading. An appetite for personalities developed, and these derogatory remarks ordinarily led to personal encounters. The streets became battle-grounds of bowie-knives and revolvers, as rivals hunted each other out. This picture may seem lurid and exaggerated, but the cold statistics of the time supply all the details.

The politicians of the day were essentially fighting men. The large majority were low-grade Southerners who had left their section, urged by unmistakable hints from their fellow-citizens. The political life of early California was colored very largely by the pseudo-chivalry which these people used as a cloak. They used the Southern code for their purposes very thoroughly, and bullied their way through society in a swashbuckling manner that could not but arouse admiration. There were many excellent Southerners in California in those days, but from the very start their influence was overshadowed by the more unworthy.

Unfortunately, later many of the better class of Southerners, yielding to prejudice and sectional feeling, joined the so-called "Law and Order" party.

It must be remembered, however, that whereas the active merchants and industrious citizens were too busy to attend to local politics, the professional low-class Southern politician had come out to California for no other purpose. To be successful, he had to be a fighting man. His revolver and his bowie-knife were part of his essential equipment. He used the word "honor" as a weapon of defense, and battered down opposition in the most high-mannered fashion by the simple expedient of claiming that he had been insulted. The fire-eater was numerous in those days. He dressed well, had good manners and appearance, possessed abundant leisure, and looked down scornfully on those citizens who were busy building the city, "low Yankee shopkeepers" being his favorite epithet.

Examined at close range, in contemporary documents, this individual has about him little of romance and nothing whatever admirable. It would be a great pity, were mistaken sentimentality allowed to clothe him in the same bright-hued garments as the cavaliers of England in the time of the Stuarts. It would be an equal pity, were the casual reader to condemn all who eventually aligned themselves against the Vigilance movement as of the same stripe as the criminals who menaced society. There were many worthy people whose education thoroughly inclined them towards formal law, and who, therefore, when the actual break came, found themselves supporting law instead of justice.

As long as the country continued to enjoy the full flood of prosperity, these things did not greatly matter. The time was individualistic, and every man was supposed to take care of himself. But in the year 1855 financial stringency overtook the new community. For lack of water many of the miners had stopped work and had to ask for credit in buying their daily necessities. The country stores had to have credit from the city because the miners could not pay, and the wholesalers of the city again had to ask extension from the East until their bills were met by the retailers. The gold of the country went East to pay its bills. Further to complicate the matter, all banking was at this time done by private firms. These could take deposits and make loans and could issue exchange, but they could not issue bank-notes. Therefore the currency was absolutely inelastic.

Even these conditions failed to shake the public optimism, until out of a clear sky came announcement that

Adams and Company had failed. Adams and Company occupied in men's minds much the same position as the Bank of England. If Adams and Company were vulnerable, then nobody was secure. The assets of the bankrupt firm were turned over to one Alfred Cohen as receiver, with whom Jones, a member of the firm of Palmer, Cook, and Company, and a third individual were associated as assignees. On petition of other creditors the judge of the district court removed Cohen and appointed one Naglee in his place. This new man, Naglee, on asking for the assets was told that they had been deposited with Palmer, Cook, and Company. The latter firm refused to give them up, denying Naglee's jurisdiction in the matter. Naglee then commenced suit against the assignees and obtained a judgment against them for $269,000. On their refusal to pay over this sum, Jones and Cohen were taken into custody. But Palmer, Cook, and Company influenced the courts, as did about every large mercantile or political firm. They soon secured the release of the prisoners, and in the general scramble for the assets of Adams and Company they secured the lion's share.

It was the same old story. An immense amount of money had disappeared. Nobody had been punished, and it was all strictly legal. Failures resulted right and left. Even Wells, Fargo, and Company closed their doors but reopened them within a few days. There was much excitement which would probably have died as other excitement had died before, had not the times produced a voice of compelling power. This voice spoke through an individual known as James King of William.

King was a man of keen mind and dauntless courage, who had tried his luck briefly at the mines, realized that the physical work was too much for him, and had therefore returned to mercantile and banking pursuits in San Francisco. His peculiar name was said to be due to the fact that at the age of sixteen, finding another James King in his immediate circle, he had added his father's name as a distinguishing mark. He was rarely mentioned except with the full designation—James King of William. On his return he opened a private banking-house, brought out his family, and entered the life of the town. For a time his banking career prospered and he acquired a moderate fortune, but in 1854 unwise investments forced him to close his office. In a high-minded fashion, very unusual in those times and even now somewhat rare, he surrendered to his creditors everything on earth he possessed. He then accepted a salaried position with Adams and Company, which he held until that house also failed. Since to the outside world his connection with the firm looked dubious, he exonerated himself through a series of pamphlets and short newspaper articles. The vigor and force of their style arrested attention, so that when his dauntless crusading spirit, revolting against the carnival of crime both subtle and obvious, desired to edit a newspaper, he had no difficulty in raising the small sum of money necessary. He had always expressed his opinions clearly and fearlessly, and the public watched with the greatest interest the appearance of the new sheet.

The first number of the *Daily Evening Bulletin* appeared on October 8, 1855. Like all papers of that day and like many of the English papers now, its first page was completely covered with small advertisements. A thin driblet of local items occupied a column on the third and fourth pages, and a single column of editorials ran down the second. As a newspaper it seemed beneath contempt, but the editorials made men sit up and take notice. King started with an attack on Palmer, Cook, and Company's methods. He said nothing whatever about the robberies. He dealt exclusively with the excessive rentals for postal boxes charged the public by Palmer, Cook, and Company. That seemed a comparatively small and harmless matter, but King made it interesting by mentioning exact names, recording specific instances, avoiding any generalities, and stating plainly that this was merely a beginning in the exposure of methods. Jones of Palmer, Cook, and Company—that same Jones who had been arrested with Cohen—immediately visited King in his office with the object of either intimidating or bribing him as the circumstances seemed to advise. He bragged of horsewhips and duels, but returned rather noncommittal. The next evening the *Bulletin* reported Jones's visit simply as an item of news, faithfully, sarcastically, and in a pompous vein. There followed no comment whatever. The next number, now eagerly purchased by every one, was more interesting because of its hints of future disclosures rather than because of its actual information. One of the alleged scoundrels was mentioned by name, and then the subject was dropped. The attention of the City Marshal was curtly called to disorderly houses and the statutes concerning them, and it was added "for his information" that at a certain address, which was given, a structure was then actually being built for improper purposes.

Then, without transition, followed a list of official bonds and sureties for which Palmer, Cook, and Company were giving vouchers, amounting to over two millions. There were no comments on this list, but the inference was obvious that the firm had the whip-hand over many public officials.

The position of the new paper was soon formally established. It possessed a large subscription list; it was eagerly bought on its appearance in the street; and its advertising was increasing. King again turned his attention to Palmer, Cook, and Company. Each day he explored succinctly, clearly, without rhetoric, some single branch of their business. By the time he had finished with them, he had not only exposed all their iniquities, but he had, which was more important, educated the public to the financial methods of the time. It followed naturally in this type of exposure that King should criticize some of the legal subterfuges, which in turn brought him to analysis of the firm's legal advisers, who had previously enjoyed a good reputation. From such subjects he drifted to dueling, venal newspapers, and soon down to the ordinary criminals such as Billy Mulligan, Wooley Kearny, Casey, Cora, Yankee Sullivan, Ned McGowan, Charles Duane, and many others. Never did he hesitate to specify names and instances. He never dealt in innuendoes. This was bringing him very close to personal danger, for worthies of the class last mentioned were the sort who carried their pistols and bowie-knives prominently displayed and handy for use. As yet no actual violence had been attempted against him. Other methods of reprisal that came to his notice, King published without comment as items of news.

Mere threats had little effect in intimidating the editor. More serious means were tried. A dozen men publicly announced that they intended to kill him—and the records of the dozen were pretty good testimonials to their sincerity. In the gambling resorts and on the streets bets were made and pools formed on the probable duration of King's life. As was his custom, he commented even upon this. Said the *Bulletin's* editorial columns: "Bets are now being offered, we have been told, that the editor of the *Bulletin* will not be in existence twenty days longer. And the case of Dr. Hogan of the Vicksburg paper who was murdered by gamblers of that place is cited as a warning. Pah!... War then is the cry, is it? War between the prostitutes and gamblers on one side and the virtuous and respectable on the other! Be it so, then! Gamblers of San Francisco, you have made your election and we are ready on our side for the issue!"

A man named Selover sent a challenge to King. King took this occasion to announce that he would consider no challenges and would fight no duels.

Selover then announced his intention of killing King on sight. Says the *Bulletin:* "Mr. Selover, it is said, carries a knife. We carry a pistol. We hope neither will be required, but if this rencontre cannot be avoided, why will Mr. Selover persist in imperiling the lives of others? We pass every afternoon about half-past four to five o'clock along Market Street from Fourth to Fifth Streets. The road is wide and not so much frequented as those streets farther in town. If we are to be shot or cut to pieces, for heaven's sake let it be done there. Others will not be injured, and in case we fall our house is but a few hundred yards beyond and the cemetery not much farther."

Boldness such as this did not act exactly as a soporific. About this time was perpetrated a crime of violence no worse than many hundreds which had preceded it, but occurring at a psychological time.

A gambler named Charles Cora shot and killed William Richardson, a United States marshal. The shooting was cold-blooded and without danger to the murderer, for at the time Richardson was unarmed. Cora was at once hustled to jail, not so much for confinement as for safety against a possible momentary public anger. Men had been shot on the street before--many men, some of them as well known and as well liked as Richardson—but not since public sentiment had been aroused and educated as the *Bulletin* had aroused and educated it. Crowds commenced at once to gather. Some talk of lynching went about. Men made violent street-corner speeches. The mobs finally surged to the jail, but were firmly met by a strong armed guard and fell back. There was much destructive and angry talk.

But to swing a mob into action there must be determined men at its head, and this mob had no leader. Sam Brannan started to say something, but was promptly arrested for inciting riot. Though the situation was ticklish, the police seem to have handled it well, making only a passive opposition and leaving the crowd to fritter its energies in purposeless cursing, surging to and fro, and harmless threatenings. Nevertheless this crowd persisted longer than most of them.

The next day the *Bulletin* vigorously counseled dependence upon the law, expressed confidence in the judges who were to try the case—Hager and Norton—and voiced a personal belief that the day had passed when it would ever be necessary to resort to arbitrary measures. It may hence be seen how far from a contemplation of extra legal measures was King in his public attitude. Nevertheless he added a paragraph of warning: "Hang Billy Mulligan—that's the word. If Mr. Sheriff Scannell does not remove Billy Mulligan from his present post as keeper of the County Jail and Mulligan lets Cora escape, hang Billy Mulligan, and if necessary to get rid of the sheriff, hang him—hang the sheriff!"

Public excitement died. Conviction seemed absolutely certain. Richardson had been a public official and a popular one. Cora's action had been cold-blooded and apparently without provocation. Nevertheless he had remained undisturbed. He had retained one of the most brilliant lawyers of the time, James McDougall. McDougall added to his staff the most able of the younger lawyers of the city. Immense sums of money were available. The source is not exactly known, but a certain Belle Cora, a prostitute afterwards married by Cora, was advancing large amounts. A man named James Casey, bound by some mysterious obligation, was active in taking up general collections. Cora lived in great luxury at the jail. He had long been a close personal friend of the sheriff and his deputy, Mulligan. When the case came to trial, Cora escaped conviction through the disagreement of the jury.

This fiasco, following King's editorials, had a profound effect on the public mind. King took the outrage against justice as a fresh starting-point for new attacks. He assailed bitterly and fearlessly the countless abuses of the time, until at last he was recognized as a dangerous opponent by the heretofore cynically amused higher criminals.

Many rumors of plots against King's life are to be found in the detailed history of the day. Whether his final assassination was the result of one of these plots, or simply the outcome of a burst of passion, matters little. Ultimately it had its source in the ungoverned spirit of the times.

Four months after the farce of the Cora trial, on May 14, King published an attack on the appointment of a certain man to a position in the federal custom house. The candidate had happened to be involved with James P. Casey in a disgraceful election. Casey was at that time one of the supervisors. Incidental to his attack on the candidate, King wrote as follows: "It does not matter how bad a man Casey had been, or how much benefit it might be to the public to have him out of the way, we cannot accord to any one citizen the right to kill him or even beat him, without justifiable provocation. The fact that Casey has been an inmate of Sing Sing prison in New York is no offense against the laws of this State; nor is the fact of his having stuffed himself through the ballot box, as elected to the Board of Supervisors from a district where it is said he was not even a candidate, any justification for Mr. Bagley to shoot Casey, however richly the latter may deserve to have his neck stretched for such fraud on the people."

Casey read this editorial in full knowledge that thousands of his fellow-citizens would also read it. He was at that time, in addition to his numerous political cares, editor of a small newspaper called *The Sunday Times*. This had been floated for the express purpose of supporting the extremists of the legalists' party, which, as we have explained, now included the gambling and lawless element. How valuable he was considered is shown by the fact that at a previous election Casey had been returned as elected supervisor, although he had not been a candidate, his name had not been on the ticket, and subsequent private investigations could unearth no man who would acknowledge having voted for him. Indeed, he was not even a resident of that district. However, a slick politician named Yankee Sullivan, who ran the election, said officially that the most votes had been counted for him; and so his election was announced. Casey was a handy tool in many ways, rarely appearing in person but adept in selecting suitable agents. He was personally popular. In appearance he is described as a short, slight man with a keen face, a good forehead, a thin but florid countenance, dark curly hair, and blue eyes; a type of unscrupulous Irish adventurer, with perhaps the dash of romantic idealism sometimes found in the worst scoundrels. Like most of his confreres, he was particularly touchy on the subject of his "honor."

On reading the *Bulletin* editorials, he proceeded at once to King's office, announcing his intention of shooting the editor on sight. Probably he would have done so except for the accidental circumstance that King happened to be busy at a table with his back turned squarely to the door. Even Casey could not shoot a man in the back, without a word of warning. He was stuttering and excited. The interview was overheard by two men in an adjoining office.

"What do you mean by that article?" cried Casey.

"What article?" asked King.

"That which says I was formerly an inmate of Sing Sing."

"Is it not true?" asked King quietly.

"That is not the question. I don't wish my past acts raked up. On that point I am sensitive."

A slight pause ensued.

"Are you done?" asked King quietly. Then leaping from the chair he burst suddenly into excitement. "There's the door, go! And never show your face here again."

Casey had lost his advantage. At the door he gathered himself together again.

"I'll say in my paper what I please," he asserted with a show of bravado. King was again in control of himself.

"You have a perfect right to do so," he rejoined. "I shall never notice your paper." Casey struck himself on the breast. "And if necessary I shall defend myself," he cried.

King bounded again from his seat, livid with anger. "Go," he commanded sharply, and Casey went.

Outside in the street Casey found a crowd waiting. The news of his visit to the *Bulletin* office had spread. His personal friends crowded around asking eager questions. Casey answered with vague generalities: he wasn't a man to be trifled with, and some people had to find out!

Blackmailing was not a healthy occupation when it aimed at a gentleman! He left the general impression that King had apologized. Bragging in this manner, Casey led the way to the Bank Exchange, the fashionable bar not far distant. Here he remained drinking and boasting for some time.

In the group that surrounded him was a certain Judge Edward McGowan, a jolly, hard-drinking, noisy individual. He had been formerly a fugitive from justice. However, through the attractions of a gay life, a combination of bullying and intrigue, he had made himself a place in the new city and had at last risen to the bench. He was apparently easy to fathom, but the stream really ran deep. Some historians claim that he had furnished King the document which proved Casey an ex-convict. It is certain that now he had great influence with Casey, and that he drew him aside from the bar and talked with him some time in a low voice. Some people insist that he furnished the navy revolver with which a few moments later Casey shot King. This may be so, but every man went armed in those days, especially men of Casey's stamp.

It is certain, however, that after his interview with McGowan, Casey took his place across the street from the Bank Exchange. There, wrapped in his cloak, he awaited King's usual promenade home.

That for some time his intention was well known is proved by the group that little by little gathered on the opposite side of the street. It is a matter of record that a small boy passing by was commandeered and sent with a message for Peter Wrightman, a deputy sheriff. Pete, out of breath, soon joined the group. There he idled, also watching,—an official charged with the maintenance of the law of the land!

At just five o'clock King turned the corner, his head bent. He started to cross the street diagonally and had almost reached the opposite sidewalk when he was confronted by Casey who stepped forward from his place of concealment behind a wagon.

"Come on," he said, throwing back his cloak, and immediately fired.

King, who could not have known what Casey was saying, was shot through the left breast, staggered, and fell. Casey then took several steps toward his victim, looked at him closely as though to be sure he had done a good job, let down the hammer of his pistol, picked up his cloak, and started for the police-station. All he wanted now was a trial under the law.

The distance to the station-house was less than a block. Instantly at the sound of the shot his friends rose about him and guarded him to the shelter of the lock-up. But at last the public was aroused. Casey had unwittingly cut down a symbol of the better element, as well as a fearless and noble man. Someone rang the old Monumental Engine House bell—the bell that had been used to call together the Vigilantes of 1851. The news spread about the city like wildfire. An immense mob appeared to spring from nowhere.

The police officials were no fools; they recognized the quality of the approaching hurricane. The city jail was too weak a structure. It was desirable to move the prisoner at once to the county jail for safe-keeping. A carriage was brought to the entrance of an alley next the city jail; the prisoner, closely surrounded by armed men, was rushed to it; and the vehicle charged out through the crowd. The mob, as yet unorganized, recoiled instinctively before the plunging horses and the presented pistols. Before anybody could gather his wits, the equipage had disappeared.

The mob surged after the disappearing vehicle, and so ended up finally in the wide open space before the county jail. The latter was a solidly built one-story building situated on top of a low cliff.

North, the marshal, had drawn up his armed men. The mob, very excited, vociferated, surging back and forth, though they did not rush, because as yet they had no leaders. Attempts were made to harangue the gathering, but everywhere the speeches were cut short. At a crucial moment the militia appeared. The crowd thought at first that the volunteer troops were coming to uphold their own side, but were soon undeceived. The troops deployed in front of the jail and stood at guard. Just then the mayor attempted to address the crowd.

"You are here creating an excitement," he said, "which may lead to occurrences this night which will require years to wipe out. You are now laboring under great excitement and I advise you to quietly disperse. I assure you the prisoner is safe. Let the law have its course and justice will be done."

He was listened to with respect, up to this point, but here arose such a chorus of jeers that he retired hastily.

"How about Richardson?" they demanded of him. "Where is the law in Cora's case? To hell with such justice!"

More and more soldiers came into the square, which was soon filled with bayonets. The favorable moment had passed and this particular crisis was, like all the other similar crises, quickly over. But the city was aroused. Mass meetings were held in the Plaza and in other convenient localities. Many meetings took place in rooms in different parts of the city. Men armed by the thousands. Vehement orators held forth from every balcony. Some of these people were, as a chronicler of the times quaintly expressed it, "considerably tight." There was great diversity of opinion. All night the city seethed with ill-directed activity. But men felt helpless and hopeless for want of efficient organization.

The so-called Southern chivalry called this affair a "fight." Indeed the *Herald* in its issue of the next morning, mistaking utterly the times, held boldly along the way of its sympathies. It also spoke of the assassination as an "affray," and stated emphatically its opinion that, "now that justice is regularly administered," there was no excuse for even the threat of public violence. This utter blindness to the meaning of the new movement and the far-reaching effect of King's previous campaign proved fatal to the paper. It declined immediately. In the meantime, attended by his wife and a whole score of volunteer physicians, King, lying in a room in the Montgomery block, was making a fight for his life.

Then people began to notice a small advertisement on the first page of the morning papers, headed *The Vigilance Committee.*

"The members of the Vigilance Committee in good standing will please meet at number 105-1/2 Sacramento Street, this day, Thursday, fifteenth instant, at nine o'clock A.M. By order of the COMMITTEE OF THIRTEEN."

People stood still in the streets, when this notice met the eye. If this was actually the old Committee of 1851, it meant business. There was but one way to find out and that was to go and see. Number 105-1/2 Sacramento Street was a three-story barn-like structure that had been built by a short-lived political party called the "Know-Nothings." The crowd poured into the hall to its full capacity, jammed the entrance ways, and gathered for blocks in the street. There all waited patiently to see what would happen.

Meantime, in the small room back of the stage, about a score of men gathered. Chief among all stood William T. Coleman. He had taken a prominent part in the old Committee of '51. With him were Clancey Dempster, small and mild of manner, blue-eyed, the last man in the room one would have picked for great stamina and courage, yet playing one of the leading roles in this crisis; the merchant Truett, towering above all the rest; Farwell, direct, uncompromising, inspired with tremendous single-minded earnestness; James Dows, of the rough and ready, humorous, blasphemous, horse-sense type; Hossefross, of the Committee of '51; Dr. Beverly Cole, high-spirited, distinguished-looking, and courtly; Isaac Bluxome, whose signature of "33 Secretary" was to become terrible, and who also had served well in 1851. These and many more of their type were considering the question dispassionately and earnestly.

"It is a serious business," said Coleman, summing up. "It is no child's play. It may prove very serious. We may get through quickly and safely, or we may so involve ourselves as never to get through."

"The issue is not one of choice but of expediency," replied Dempster. "Shall we have vigilance with order or a mob with anarchy?"

In this spirit Coleman addressed the crowd waiting in the large hall. "In view of the miscarriage of justice in the courts," he announced briefly, "it has been thought expedient to revive the Vigilance Committee. An Executive Council should be chosen, representative of the whole body. I have been asked to take charge. I will do so, but must stipulate that I am to be free to choose the first council myself. Is that agreed?"

He received a roar of assent.

"Very well, gentlemen, I shall request you to vacate the hall. In a short time the books will be open for enrollment."

With almost disciplined docility the crowd arose and filed out, joining the other crowd waiting patiently in the street.

After a remarkably short period the doors were again thrown open. Inside the passage stood twelve men later to be known as the Executive Committee. These held back the rush, admitting but one man at a time. The crowd immediately caught the idea and helped. There was absolutely no excitement. Every man seemed grimly in earnest. Cries of "Order, order, line up!" came all down the street. A rough queue was formed.

There were no jokes or laughing; there was even no talk. Each waited his turn. At the entrance every applicant was closely scrutinized and interrogated. Several men were turned back peremptorily in the first few minutes, with the warning not to dare make another attempt. Passed by this Committee, the candidate climbed the stairs. In the second story behind a table sat Coleman, Dempster, and one other. These administered to him an oath of secrecy and then passed him into another room where sat Bluxome behind a ledger. Here his name was written and he was assigned a number by which henceforth in the activities of the Committee he was to be known. Members were instructed always to use numbers and never names in referring to other members.

Those who had been enrolled waited for some time, but finding that with evening the applicants were still coming in a long procession, they gradually dispersed. No man, however, departed far from the vicinity.

Short absences and hastily snatched meals were followed by hurried returns, lest something be missed. From time to time rumors were put in circulation as to the activities of the Executive Committee, which had been in continuous session since its appointment. An Examining

Committee had been appointed to scrutinize the applicants. The number of the Executive Committee had been raised to twenty-six; a Chief of Police had been chosen, and he in turn appointed messengers and policemen, who set out in search of individuals wanted as door-keepers, guards, and so forth. Only registered members were allowed on the floor of the hall. Even the newspaper reporters were gently but firmly ejected. There was no excitement or impatience.

At length, at eight o'clock, Coleman came out of one of the side-rooms and, mounting a table, called for order. He explained that a military organization had been decided upon, advised that numbers 1 to 100 inclusive should assemble in one corner of the room, the second hundred at the first window, and so on. An interesting order was his last. "Let the French assemble in the middle of the hall," he said in their language—an order significant of the great numbers of French who had first answered the call of gold in '49, and who now with equal enthusiasm answered the call for essential justice. Each company was advised to elect its own officers, subject to ratification by the Executive Committee. It was further stated that arrangements had been made to hire muskets to the number of several thousands from one George Law. These were only flintlocks, but efficient enough in their way, and supplied with bayonets. They were discarded government weapons, brought out some time ago by Law to arm some mysterious filibustering expedition that had fallen through. In this manner, without confusion, an organization of two thousand men was formed—sixteen military companies.

By Saturday morning, May 17, the Committee rooms were overwhelmed by crowds of citizens who desired to be enrolled. Larger quarters had already been secured in a building on the south side of Sacramento Street. Thither the Committee now removed *en masse*, without interrupting their labors. These new headquarters soon became famous in the history of this eventful year.

In the meantime the representatives of the law had not been less alert. The regular police force was largely increased. The sheriff issued thousands of summonses calling upon citizens for service as deputies.

These summonses were made out in due form of law. To refuse them meant to put oneself outside the law. The ordinary citizen was somewhat puzzled by the situation. A great many responded to the appeal from force of habit. Once they accepted the oath these new deputies were confronted by the choice between perjury, and its consequences, or doing service. On the other hand, the issue of the summonses forced many otherwise neutral men into the ranks of the Vigilantes. If they refused to act when directly summoned by law, that very fact placed them on the wrong side of the law. Therefore they felt that joining a party pledged to what practically amounted to civil war was only a short step further.

Against these the various military companies were mustered, reminded of their oath, called upon to fulfill their sworn duty, and sent to various strategic points about the jail and elsewhere. The Governor was informally notified of a state of insurrection and was requested to send in the state militia. By evening all the forces of organized society were under arms, and the result was a formidable, apparently impregnable force.

Nor was the widespread indignation against the shooting of James King of William entirely unalloyed by bitterness. King had been a hard hitter, an honest man, a true crusader; but in the heat of battle he had not always had time to make distinctions. Thus he had quite justly attacked the *Times* and other venal newspapers, but in so doing had, by too general statements, drawn the fire of every other journal in town. He had attacked with entire reason a certain Catholic priest, a man the Church itself would probably soon have disciplined, but in so doing had managed to enrage all Roman Catholics. In like manner his scorn of the so-called "chivalry" was certainly well justified, but his manner of expression offended even the best Southerners. Most of us see no farther than the immediate logic of the situation. Those perfectly worthy citizens were inclined to view the Vigilantes, not as a protest against intolerable conditions, but rather as personal champions of King.

In thus relying on the strength of their position the upholders of law realized that there might be fighting, and even severe fighting, but it must be remembered that the Law and Order party loved fighting. It was part of their education and of their pleasure and code. No wonder that they viewed with equanimity and perhaps with joy the beginning of the Vigilance movement of 1856.

The leaders of the Law and Order party chose as their military commander William Tecumseh Sherman, whose professional ability and integrity in later life are unquestioned, but whose military genius was equaled only by his extreme inability to remember facts. When writing his *Memoirs*, the General evidently forgot that original documents existed or that statements concerning historical events can often be checked up. A mere mob is irresponsible and anonymous. But it was not a mob with whom Sherman was faced, for, as a final satisfaction to the legal-minded, the men of the Vigilance Committee had put down their names on record as responsible for this movement, and it is upon contemporary record that the story of these eventful days must rely for its details.

Chapter Fourteen: The Storm Breaks

The Governor of the State at this time was J. Neely Johnson, a politician whose merits and demerits were both so slight that he would long since have been forgotten were it not for the fact that he occupied office during this excitement. His whole life heretofore had been one of trimming. He had made his way by this method, and he gained the Governor's chair by yielding to the opinion of others. He took his color and his temporary belief from those with whom he happened to be. His judgment often stuck at trifles, and his opinions were quickly heated but as quickly cooled. The added fact that his private morals were not above criticism gave men an added hold over him.

On receipt of the request for the state militia by the law party, but not by the proper authorities. Governor Johnson hurried down from Sacramento to San Francisco. Immediately on arriving in the city he sent word to Coleman requesting an interview.

Coleman at once visited him at his hotel. Johnson apparently made every effort to appear amiable and conciliatory. In answer to all questions Coleman replied: "We want peace, and if possible without a struggle."

"It is all very well," said Johnson, "to talk about peace with an army of insurrection newly raised. But what is it you actually wish to accomplish?"

"The law is crippled," replied Coleman. "We want merely to accomplish what the crippled law should do but cannot. This done, we will gladly retire. Now you have been asked by the mayor and certain others to bring out the militia and crush this movement. I assure you it cannot be done, and, if you attempt it, it will cause you and us great trouble. Do as Governor McDougal did in '51. See in this movement what he saw in that—a local movement for a local reform in which the State is not concerned. We are not a mob. We demand no overthrow of institutions. We ask not a single court to adjourn. We ask not a single officer to vacate his position. We demand only the enforcement of the law which we have made."

This expression of intention, with a little elaboration and argument, fired Johnson to enthusiasm. He gave his full support, unofficially of course, to the movement.

"But," he concluded, "hasten the undertaking as much as you can. The opposition is stronger than you suppose. The pressure on me is going to be terrible. What about the prisoners in the jail?"

Coleman evaded this last question by saying that the matter was in the hands of the Committee, and he then left the Governor.

Coleman at once returned to headquarters where the Executive Committee was in session, getting rid of its routine business. After a dozen matters were settled, it was moved "that the Committee as a body shall visit the county jail at such time as the Executive Committee might direct, and take thence James P. Casey and Charles Cora, give them a fair trial, and administer such punishment as justice shall demand."

This, of course, was the real business for which all this organization had been planned. A moment's pause succeeded the proposal, but an instantaneous and unanimous assent followed the demand for a vote. At this precise instant a messenger opened the door and informed them that Governor Johnson was in the building requesting speech with Coleman.

Coleman found Johnson, accompanied by Sherman and a few others, lounging in the anteroom. The Governor sprawled in a chair, his hat pulled over his eyes, a cigar in the corner of his mouth. His companions arose and bowed gravely as Coleman entered the room, but the Governor remained seated and nodded curtly with an air of bravado. Without waiting for even the ordinary courtesies he burst out. "We have come to ask what you intend to do," he demanded.

Coleman, thoroughly surprised, with the full belief that the subject had all been settled in the previous interview, replied curtly. "I agree with you as to the grievances," rejoined the Governor, "but the courts are the proper remedy. The judges are good men, and there is no necessity for the people to turn themselves into a mob."

"Sir!" cried Coleman. "This is no mob!—You know this is no mob!"

The Governor went on to explain that it might become necessary to bring out all the force at his command. Coleman, though considerably taken aback, recovered himself and listened without comment. He realized that Sherman and the other men were present as witnesses. "I will report your remark to my associates," he contented himself with saying. The question of witnesses, however, bothered Coleman. He darted in to the committee room and shortly returned with witnesses of his own.

"Let us now understand each other clearly," he resumed. "As I understand your proposal, it is that, if we make no move, you guarantee no escape, an immediate trial, and instant execution?"

Johnson agreed to this.

"We doubt your ability to do this," went on Coleman, "but we are ready to meet you half-way. This is what we will promise: we will take no steps without first giving you notice. But in return we insist that ten men of our own selection shall be added to the sheriff's force within the jail."

Johnson, who was greatly relieved and delighted, at once agreed to this proposal, and soon withdrew. But the blunder he had made was evident enough. With Coleman, who was completely outside the law, he, as an executive of the law, had no business treating or making agreements at all. Furthermore, as executive of the State, he had no legal right to interfere with city affairs unless he were formally summoned by the authorities. Up to now he had merely been notified by private citizens. And to cap the whole sheaf of blunders, he had now in this private interview treated with rebels, and to their advantage. For, as Coleman probably knew, the last agreement was all for the benefit of the Committee. They gained the right to place a personal guard over the prisoners. They gave in return practically only a promise to withdraw that guard before attacking the jail—a procedure which was eminently practical if they cared anything for the safety of the guard.

Johnson was thoroughly pleased with himself until he reached the hotel where the leaders of the opposition were awaiting him. Their keen legal minds saw at once the position in which he had placed himself. After a hasty discussion, it was decided to claim that the Committee had waived all right of action, and that they had promised definitely to leave the case to the courts.

When this statement had been industriously circulated and Coleman had heard of it, he is said to have exclaimed: "The time has come. After that, it is either ourselves or a mob."

He proceeded at once to the Vigilance headquarters and summoned Olney, the appointed guardian of the jail. Him he commanded to get together sixty of the best men possible. A call was sent out for the companies to assemble. They soon began to gather, coming some in rank as they had gathered in their headquarters outside, others singly and in groups. Doorkeepers prevented all exit: once a man was in, he was not permitted to go out. Each leader received explicit directions as to what was to be done. He was instructed as to precisely when he and his command were to start; from what given point; along exactly what route to proceed; and at just what time to arrive at a given point—not a moment sooner or later. The plan for concerted action was very carefully and skillfully worked out. Olney's sixty men were instructed to lay aside their muskets and, armed only with pistols, to make their way by different routes to the jail.

Sunday morning dawned fair and calm. But as the day wore on, an air of unrest pervaded the city. Rumors of impending action were already abroad. The jail itself hummed like a hive. Men came and went, busily running errands, and darting about through the open door. Armed men were taking their places on the flat roof. Meantime the populace gathered slowly. At first there were only a score or so idling around the square; but little by little they increased in numbers. Black forms began to appear on the rooftops all about; white faces showed at the windows; soon the center of the square had filled; the converging streets became black with closely packed people. The windows and doors and balconies, the copings and railings, the slopes of the hills round about were all occupied. In less than an hour twenty thousand people had gathered. They took their positions quietly and waited patiently. It was evident that they had assembled in the role of spectators only, and that action had been left to more competent and better organized men. There was no shouting, no demonstration, and so little talking that it amounted only to a low murmur. Already the doors of the jail had been closed. The armed forces on the roof had been increased.

After a time the congested crowd down one of the side-streets was agitated by the approach of a body of armed men. At the same instant a similar group began to appear at the end of another and converging street. The columns came steadily forward, as the people gave way. The men wore no uniforms, and the glittering steel of their bayonets furnished the only military touch. The two columns reached the convergence of the street at the same time and as they entered the square before the jail a third and a fourth column debouched from other directions, while still others deployed into view on the hills behind.

They all took their places in rank around the square. Among the well-known characters of the times was a certain Colonel Gift. Mr. Hubert H. Bancroft, the chronicler of these events, describes him as "a tall, lank, empty-boweled, tobacco-spurting Southerner, with eyes like burning black balls, who could talk a company of listeners into an insane asylum quicker than any man in California, and whose blasphemy could not be equaled, either in quantity or quality, by the most profane of any age or nation." He remarked to a friend nearby, as he watched the spectacle below: "When you see these damned psalm-singing Yankees turn out of their churches, shoulder their guns, and march away of a Sunday, you may know that hell is going to crack shortly."

For some time the armed men stood rigid, four deep all around the square. Behind them the masses of the people watched. Then at a command the ranks fell apart and from the side-streets marched the sixty men chosen by Olney, dragging a field gun at the end of a rope. This they wheeled into position in the square and pointed it at the door of the jail. Quite deliberately, the cannon was loaded with powder and balls. A man lit a slow match, blew it to a glow, and took his position at the breech. Nothing then happened for a full ten minutes. The six men stood rigid by the gun in the middle of the square. The sunlight gleamed from the ranks of bayonets. The vast multitude held its breath. The wall of the jail remained blank and inscrutable.

Then a man on horseback was seen to make his way through the crowd. This was Charles Doane, Grand Marshal of the Vigilantes. He rode directly to the jail door, on which he rapped with the handle of his riding-whip. After a moment the wicket in the door opened. Without dismounting, the rider handed a note within, and then, backing his horse the length of the square, came to rest.

Again the ranks parted and closed, this time to admit of three carriages. As they came to a stop, the muskets all around the square leaped to "present arms!" From the carriages descended Coleman, Truett, and several others. In dead silence they walked to the jail door, Olney's men close at their heels. For some moments they spoke through the wicket; then the door swung open and the Committee entered.

Up to this moment Casey had been fully content with the situation. He was, of course, treated to the best the jail or the city could afford.

It was a bother to have been forced to shoot James King of William; but the nuisance of incarceration for a time was a small price to pay. His friends had rallied well to his defense. He had no doubt whatever, that, according to the usual custom, he would soon work his way through the courts and stand again a free man. His first intimation of trouble was the hearing of the resonant tramp of feet outside. His second was when Sheriff Scannell stood before him with the Vigilantes' note in his hand.

Casey took one glance at Scannell's face. "You aren't going to betray me?" he cried. "You aren't going to give me up?"

"James," replied Scannell solemnly, "there are three thousand armed men coming for you and I have not thirty supporters around the jail."

"Not thirty!" cried Casey astonished. For a moment he appeared crushed; then he leaped to his feet flourishing a long knife. "I'll not be taken from this place alive!" he cried.

"Where are all you brave fellows who were going to see me through this?"

At this moment Coleman knocked at the door of the jail. The sheriff hurried away to answer the summons.

Casey took the opportunity to write a note for the Vigilantes which he gave to the marshal. It read:

"*To the Vigilante Committee.* GENTLEMEN:--I am willing to go before you if you will let me speak but ten minutes. I do not wish to have the blood of any man upon my head."

On entering the jail door Coleman and his companions bowed formally to the sheriff.

"We have come for the prisoner Casey," said Coleman. "We ask that he be peaceably delivered us handcuffed at the door immediately."

"Under existing circumstances," replied Scannell, "I shall make no resistance. The prison and its contents are yours."

But Truett would have none of this. "We want only the man Casey at present," he said. "For the safety of all the rest we hold you strictly accountable."

They proceeded at once to Casey's cell. The murderer heard them coming and sprang back from the door holding his long knife poised. Coleman walked directly to the door, where he stopped, looking Casey in the eye. At the end of a full minute he exclaimed sharply: "Lay down that knife!"

As though the unexpected tones had broken a spell, Casey flung the knife from him and buried his face in his hands. Then, and not until then, Coleman informed him curtly that his request would be granted.

They took Casey out through the door of the jail. The crowd gathered its breath for a frantic cheer. The relief from tension must have been great, but Coleman, bareheaded, raised his hand and, in instant obedience to the gesture, the cheer was stifled. The leaders then entered the carriage, which immediately turned and drove away.

Thus Casey was safely in custody. Charles Cora, who, it will be remembered, had killed Marshal Richardson and who had gained from the jury a disagreement, was taken on a second trip.

The street outside headquarters soon filled with an orderly crowd awaiting events. There was noticeable the same absence of excitement, impatience, or tumult so characteristic of the popular gatherings of that time, except perhaps when the meetings were conducted by the partisans of Law and Order.

After a long interval one of the Committee members appeared at an upper window. "It is not the intention of the Committee to be hasty," he announced. "Nothing will be done today."

This statement was received in silence. At last someone asked: "Where are Casey and Cora?"

"The Committee hold possession of the jail. All are safe," said the Committee man.

With this simple statement the crowd was completely satisfied, and dispersed quietly and at once.

Of the three thousand enrolled men, three hundred were retained under arms at headquarters, a hundred surrounded the jail, and all the rest were dismissed. Next day, Monday, headquarters still remained inscrutable; but large patrols walked about the city, collecting arms.

The gunshops were picketed and their owners were warned under no circumstances to sell weapons. Towards evening the weather grew colder and rain came on. Even this did not discourage the crowd, which stood about in its sodden clothes waiting. At midnight it reluctantly dispersed, but by daylight the following morning the streets around headquarters were blocked. Still it rained, and still apparently nothing happened. All over the city business was at a standstill. Men had dropped their affairs, even the most pressing, either to take part in this movement or to lend the moral support of their presence and their interest.

The partisans of Law and Order, so called, were also abroad. No man dared express himself in mixed company openly. The courts were empty. Some actually closed down, with one excuse or another; but most of them pretended to go through the forms of business. Many judges took the occasion to leave town—on vacation, they announced. These incidents occasioned lively comment. As our chronicler before quoted tells us: "A good many who had things on their minds left for the country." Still it rained steadily, and still the crowds waited.

The prisoners, Casey and Cora, had expected, when taken from the jail, to be lynched at once. But, since the execution had been thus long postponed, they began to take heart. They understood that they were to have a clear trial "according to law"—a phrase which was in those days immensely cheering to malefactors. They were not entirely cut off from outside communication. Casey was allowed to see several men on pressing business, and permitted to talk to them freely, although before a witness from the Committee. Cora received visits from Belle Cora, who in the past had spent thousands on his legal defense. Now she came to see him faithfully and reported every effort that was being made.

On Tuesday, the 20th, Cora was brought before the Committee. He asked for counsel, and Truett was appointed to act for him. A list of witnesses demanded by Cora was at once summoned, and a sub-committee was sent to bring them before the board of trial. All the ordinary forms of law were closely followed, and all the essential facts were separately brought out. It was the same old Cora trial over again with one modification; namely, that all technicalities and technical delays were eliminated. Not an attempt was made to confine the investigation to the technical trial. By dusk the case for the prosecution was finished, and that for the defense was supposed to begin.

During all this long interim the Executive Committee had sat in continuous session. They had agreed that no recess of more than thirty minutes should be taken until a decision had been reached. But of all the long list of witnesses submitted by Cora for the defense not one could be found. They were in hiding and afraid. The former perjurers would not appear.

It was now falling dusk. The corners of the great room were in darkness. Beneath the elevated desk, behind which sat Coleman, Bluxome, the secretary, lighted a single oil lamp, the better to see his notes. In the interest of the proceedings a general illumination had not been ordered. Within the shadow, the door opened and Charles Doane, the Grand Marshal of the Vigilantes, advanced three steps into the room.

"Mr. President," he said clearly, "I am instructed to announce that James King of William is dead."

The conviction of both men took place that night, and the execution was ordered, but in secret.

Thursday noon had been set for the funeral of James King of William. This ceremony was to take place in the Unitarian church. A great multitude had gathered to attend. The church was filled to overflowing early in the day. But thousands of people thronged the streets round about, and stood patiently and seriously to do the man honor. Historians of the time detail the names of many marching bodies from every guild and society in the new city. Hundreds of horsemen, carriages, and foot marchers got themselves quietly into the line. They also were excluded from the funeral ceremonies by lack of room, but wished to do honor to the cortège. This procession is said to have been over two miles in length. Each man wore a band of crêpe around his left arm. All the city seemed to be gathered there. And yet the time for the actual funeral ceremony was still some hours distant.

Nevertheless the few who, hurrying to the scene, had occasion to pass near the Vigilante headquarters, found the silent square guarded on all sides by a triple line of armed men. The side-streets also were filled with them. They stood in the exact alignment their constant drill had made possible, with bayonets fixed, staring straight ahead. Three thousand were under arms. Like the vast crowd a few squares away, they, too, stood silent and patiently waiting. At a quarter before one the upper windows of the headquarters building were thrown open and small planked platforms were thrust from two of them. Heavy beams were shoved out from the flat roof directly over the platforms. From the ends of the beams dangled nooses of rope. After this another wait ensued.

Across the silence of the intervening buildings could be heard faintly from the open windows of the church the sound of an organ, and then the measured cadences of an oration. The funeral services had begun.

As though this were a signal, the blinds that had closed the window openings were thrown back and Cora was conducted to the end of one of the little platforms. His face was covered with a white handkerchief and he was bound. A moment later Casey appeared. He had asked not to be blindfolded. Cora stood bolt upright, motionless as a stone, but Casey's courage broke. If he had any hope that the boastful promises of his friends would be fulfilled by a rescue, that hope died as he looked down on the set, grim faces, on the sinister ring of steel. His nerve then deserted him completely and he began to babble.

"Gentlemen," he cried at them, "I am not a murderer! I do not feel afraid to meet my God on a charge of murder! I have done nothing but what I thought was right! Whenever I was injured I have resented it! It has been part of my education during twenty-nine years! Gentlemen, I forgive you this persecution! O God! My poor Mother! O God!"

It is to be noted that he said not one word of contrition nor of regret for the man whose funeral services were then going on, nor for the heartbroken wife who knelt at that coffin. His words found no echo against that grim wall of steel. Again ensued a wait, apparently inexplicable.

Across the intervening housetops the sound of the oration ceased. At the door of the church a slight commotion was visible. The coffin was being carried out. It was placed in the hearse. Every head was bared. There followed a slight pause; then from overhead the church-bell boomed out once. Another bell in the next block answered; a third, more distant, chimed in. From all parts of the city tolled the requiem.

At the first stroke of the bell the funeral cortège moved forward toward Lone Mountain cemetery.

At the first stroke the Vigilantes as one man presented arms. The platforms dropped, and Casey and Cora fell into eternity.

Chapter Fifteen: The Vigilantes of '56

This execution naturally occasioned a great storm of indignation among the erstwhile powerful adherents of the law. The ruling, aristocratic class, the so-called chivalry, the best element of the city, had been slapped deliberately in the face, and this by a lot of Yankee shopkeepers. The Committee were stigmatized as stranglers. They ought to be punished as murderers! They should be shot down as revolutionists! It was realized, however, that the former customary street-shooting had temporarily become unsafe. Otherwise there is no doubt that brawls would have been more frequent than they were.

An undercurrent of confidence was apparent, however. The Law and Order men had been surprised and overpowered. They had yielded only to overwhelming odds. With the execution of Cora and Casey accomplished, the Committee might be expected to disband. And when the Committee disbanded, the law would have its innings. Its forces would then be better organized and consolidated, its power assured. It could then safely apprehend and bring to justice the ringleaders of this undertaking. Many of the hotheads were in favor of using armed force to take Coleman and his fellow-conspirators into custody. But calmer spirits advised moderation for the present, until the time was more ripe.

But to the surprise and indignation of these people, the Vigilantes showed no intention of disbanding. Their activities extended and their organization strengthened.

The various military companies drilled daily until they went through the manual with all the precision of regular troops. The Committee's book remained opened, and by the end of the week over seven thousand men had signed the roll. Loads of furniture and various supplies stopped at the doors of headquarters and were carried in by members of the organization. No non-member ever saw the inside of the building while it was occupied by the Committee of Vigilance. So cooking utensils, cot-beds, provisions, blankets, bulletin-boards, arms, chairs and tables, field-guns, ammunition, and many other supplies seemed to indicate a permanent occupation. Doorkeepers were always in attendance, and sentinels patrolled in the streets and on the roof.

Every day the Executive Committee was in session for all of the daylight hours. A blacklist was in preparation. Orders were issued for the Vigilante police to arrest certain men and to warn certain others to leave town immediately. A choice haul was made of the lesser lights of the ward-heelers and chief politicians. A very good sample was the notorious Yankee Sullivan, an ex-prize-fighter, ward-heeler, ballot-box stuffer, and shoulder-striker. He, it will be remembered, was the man who returned Casey as supervisor in a district where, as far as is known, Casey was not a candidate and no one could be found who had voted for him. This individual went to pieces completely shortly after his arrest. He not only confessed the details of many of his own crimes but, what was more important, disclosed valuable information as to others.

His testimony was important, not necessarily as final proof against those whom he accused, but as indication of the need of thorough investigation. Then without warning he committed suicide in his cell.

On investigation it turned out that he had been accustomed to from sixty to eighty drinks of whiskey each day, and the sudden and complete deprivation had unhinged his mind. Warned by this unforeseen circumstance, the Committee henceforth issued regular rations of whiskey to all its prisoners, a fact which is a striking commentary on the character of the latter. It is to be noted, furthermore, that liquor of all sorts was debarred from the deliberations of the Vigilantes themselves.

Trials went briskly forward in due order, with counsel for defense and ample opportunity to call witnesses. There were no more capital punishments. It was made known that the Committee had set for itself a rule that capital punishment would be inflicted by it only for crimes so punishable by the regular law. But each outgoing ship took a crowd of the banished. The majority of the first sweepings were low thugs—"Sydney Ducks," hangers-on, and the worst class of criminals; but a certain number were taken from what had been known as the city's best.

In the law courts these men would have been declared as white as the driven snow; in fact, that had actually happened to some of them. But they were plainly undesirable citizens. The Committee so decided and bade them depart. Among the names of men who were prominent and influential in the early history of the city, but who now were told to leave, were Charles Duane, Woolley Kearny, William McLean, J.D. Musgrave, Peter Wightman, James White, and Edward McGowan. Hundreds of others left the city of their own accord. Terror spread among the inhabitants of the underworld. Some of the minor offenders brought in by the Vigilante police were turned over by the Executive Committee to the regular law courts. It is significant that, whereas convictions had been almost unknown up to this time, every one of these offenders was promptly sentenced by those courts.

But though the underworld was more or less terrified, the upper grades were only the further aroused. Many sincerely believed that this movement was successful only because it was organized, that the people of the city were scattered and powerless, that they needed only to be organized to combat the forces of disorder. In pursuance of the belief that the public at large needed merely to be called together loyally to defend its institutions, a meeting was set for June 2, in Portsmouth Square. Elaborate secret preparations, including the distribution of armed men, were made to prevent interference. Such preparations were useless. Immediately after the appearance of the notice the Committee of Vigilance issued orders that the meeting was to be in no manner discouraged or molested.

It was well attended. Enormous crowds gathered, not only in and around the Square itself, but in balconies and windows and on housetops. It was a very disrespectful crowd, evidently out for a good time.

On the platform within the Square stood or sat the owners of many of the city's proud names. Among them were well-known speakers, men who had never failed to hold and influence a crowd. But only a short distance away little could be heard. It early became evident that, though there would be no interference, the sentiment of the crowd was adverse. And what must have been particularly maddening was that the sentiment was good-humored. Colonel Edward Baker came forward to speak. The Colonel was a man of great eloquence, so that in spite of his considerable lack of scruples he had won his way to a picturesque popularity and fame. But the crowd would have little of him this day, and an almost continuous uproar drowned out his efforts. The usual catch phrases, such as "liberty." "Constitution," "habeas corpus," "trial by jury," and "freedom," occasionally became audible, but the people were not interested. "See Cora's defender!" cried someone, voicing the general suspicion that Baker had been one of the little gambler's hidden counsel. "Cora!" "Ed. Baker!" "$10,000!" "Out of that, you old reprobate!" He spoke ten minutes against the storm and then yielded, red-faced and angry.

Others tried but in vain. A Southerner, Benham, inveighing passionately against the conditions of the city, in throwing back his coat happened inadvertently to reveal the butt of a Colt revolver. The bystanders immediately caught the point. "There's a pretty Law and Order man!" they shouted. "Say, Benham, don't you know it's against the law to go armed?"

"I carry this weapon," he cried, shaking his fist, "not as an instrument to overthrow the law, but to uphold it."

Someone from a balcony nearby interrupted: "In other words, sir, you break the law in order to uphold the law. What more are the Vigilantes doing?" The crowd went wild over this response. The confusion became worse.

Upholders of Law and Order thrust forward Judge Campbell in the hope that his age and authority on the bench would command respect. He was unable, however, to utter even two consecutive sentences.

"I once thought," he interrupted himself piteously, "that I was the free citizen of a free country. But recent occurrences have convinced me that I am a slave, more a slave than any on a Southern plantation, for they know their masters, but I know not mine!"

But his auditors refused to be affected by pathos.

"Oh, yes you do," they informed him. "You know your masters as well as anybody. Two of them were hanged the other day!"

Though this attempt at home to gain coherence failed, the partisans at Sacramento had better luck. They collected, it was said, five hundred men hailing from all quarters of the globe, but chiefly from the Southeast and Texas. All of them were fire-eaters, reckless, and sure to make trouble. Two pieces of artillery were reported coming down the Sacramento to aid all prisoners, but especially Billy Mulligan. The numbers were not in themselves formidable as opposed to the enrollment of the Vigilance Committee, but it must be remembered that the city was full of scattered warriors and of cowed members of the underworld waiting only leaders and a rallying point. Even were the Vigilantes to win in the long run, the material for a very pretty civil war was ready to hand. Two hundred men were hastily put to filling gunnybags with sand and to fortifying not only headquarters but the streets round about. Cannon were mounted, breastworks were piled, and embrasures were cut. By morning Fort Gunnybags, as headquarters was henceforth called, had come into existence.

The fire-eaters arrived that night, but they were not five hundred strong, as excited rumor had it. They disembarked, greeting the horde of friends who had come to meet them, marched in a body to Fort Gunnybags, looked it over, stuck their hands into their pockets, and walked peacefully away to the nearest bar-rooms. This was the wisest move on their part, for by now the disposition of the Vigilante men was so complete that nothing short of regularly organized troops could successfully have dislodged them.

Behind headquarters was a long shed and stable In which were to be found at all hours saddle horses and artillery horses, saddled and bridled, ready for instant use. Twenty-six pieces of artillery, most of them sent in by captains of vessels in the harbor, were here parked. Other cannon were mounted for the defense of the fort itself. Muskets, rifles, and sabers had been accumulated. A portable barricade had been constructed in the event of possible street fighting—a sort of wheeled framework that could be transformed into litters or scaling-ladders at will. Mess offices and kitchens were there that could feed a small army. Flags and painted signs carrying the open eye that had been adopted as emblematic of vigilance decorated the main room. A huge alarm bell had been mounted upon the roof. Mattresses, beds, cots, and other furniture necessary to accommodate whole companies on the premises themselves, had been provided. A completely equipped armorers' shop and a hospital with all supplies occupied the third story. The forces were divided into four companies of artillery, one squadron and two troops of cavalry, four regiments and thirty-two companies of infantry, besides the small but very efficient police organization. A tap on the bell gathered these men in an incredibly short space of time. Bancroft says that, as a rule, within fifteen minutes of the first stroke seven-tenths of the entire forces would be on hand ready for combat.

The Law and Order people recognized the strength of this organization and realized that they must go at the matter in a more thorough manner.

They turned their attention to the politics of the structure, and here they had every reason to hope for success. No matter how well organized the Vigilantes might be or how thoroughly they might carry the sympathies of the general public, there was no doubt that they were acting in defiance of constituted law, and therefore were nothing less than rebels. It was not only within the power, but it was also a duty, of the Governor to declare the city in a condition of insurrection. When he had done this, the state troops must put down the insurrection; and, if they failed, then the Federal Government itself should be called on.

Looked at in this way, the small handful of disturbers, no matter how well armed and disciplined, amounted to very little.

Naturally the Governor had first to be won over. Accordingly all the important men of San Francisco took the steamer *Senator* for Sacramento where they met Judge Terry, of the Supreme Court of California, Volney Howard, and others of the same ilk. No governor of Johnson's nature could long withstand such pressure. He promised to issue the required proclamation of insurrection as soon as it could be "legally proved" that the Vigilance Committee had acted outside the law. The small fact that it had already hanged two and deported a great many others, to say nothing of taking physical possession of the city, meant little to these legal minds.

In order that all things should be technically correct, then, Judge Terry issued a writ of habeas corpus for William Mulligan and gave it into the hands of Deputy Sheriff Harrison for service on the Committee.

It was expected that the Committee would deny the writ, which would constitute legal defiance of the State. The Governor would then be justified in issuing the proclamation. If the state troops proved unwilling or inadequate, as might very well be, the plan was then to call on the United States. The local representatives of the central government were at that time General Wool commanding the military department of California, and Captain David Farragut in command of the navy-yard. Within their command was a force sufficient to subdue three times the strength of the Vigilance Committee. William Tecumseh Sherman, then in private life, had been appointed major-general of a division of the state militia. As all this was strictly legal, the plan could not possibly fail.

Harrison took the writ of habeas corpus and proceeded to San Francisco. He presented himself at headquarters and offered his writ. Instead of denying it, the Committee welcomed him cordially and invited him to make a thorough search of the premises. Of course Harrison found nothing—the Committee had seen to that—and departed. The scheme had failed. The Committee had in no way denied his authority or his writ. But Harrison saw clearly what had been expected of him. To Judge Terry he unblushingly returned the writ endorsed "prevented from service by armed men." For the sake of his cause, Harrison had lied. However, the whole affair was now regarded as legal.

Johnson promptly issued his proclamation. The leaders, in high feather, as promptly turned to the federal authorities for the assistance they needed. As yet they did not ask for troops but only for weapons with which to arm their own men. To their blank dismay General Wool refused to furnish arms. He took the position that he had no right to do so without orders from Washington. There is no doubt, however, that this technical position cloaked the doughty warrior's real sympathies.

Colonel Baker and Volney Howard were instructed to wait on him. After a somewhat lengthy conversation, they made the mistake of threatening him with a report to Washington for refusing to uphold the law.

"I think, gentlemen," flashed back the veteran indignantly, "I know my duty and in its performance dread no responsibility!" He promptly bowed them out.

In the meantime the Executive Committee had been patiently working down through its blacklist. It finally announced that after June 24 it would consider no fresh cases, and a few days later it proclaimed an adjournment parade on July 4. It considered its work completed and the city safe.

It may be readily imagined that this peaceful outcome did not in the least suit the more aristocratic members of the Law and Order party. They were a haughty, individualistic, bold, forceful, sometimes charming band of fire-eaters. In their opinion they had been deeply insulted.

They wanted reprisal and punishment.

When therefore the Committee set a definite day for disbanding, the local authorities and upholders of law were distinctly disappointed.

They saw slipping away the last chance for a clash of arms that would put these rebels in their places. There was some thought of arresting the ringleaders, but the courts were by now so well terrorized that it was by no means certain that justice as defined by the Law and Order party could be accomplished. And even if conviction could be secured, the representatives of the law found little satisfaction in ordinary punishment. What they wanted was a fight.

General Sherman had resigned his command of the military forces in disgust. In his stead was chosen General Volney Howard, a man typical of his class, blinded by his prejudices and his passions, filled with a sense of the importance of his caste, and without grasp of the broader aspects of the situation. In the Committee's present attitude he saw not the signs of a job well done, but indications of weakening, and he considered this a propitious moment to show his power. In this attitude he received enthusiastic backing from Judge Terry and his narrow coterie. Terry was then judge of the Supreme Court; and a man more unfitted for the position it would be difficult to find. A tall, attractive, fire-eating Texan with a charming wife, he stood high in the social life of the city. His temper was undisciplined and completely governed his judgment. Intensely partisan and, as usual with his class, touchy on the point of honor, he did precisely the wrong thing on every occasion where cool decision was demanded.

It was so now. The Law and Order party persuaded Governor Johnson to order a parade of state troops in the streets of San Francisco. The argument used was that such a parade of legally organized forces would overawe the citizens. The secret hope, however, which was well founded, was that such a display would promote the desired conflict. This hope they shared with Howard, after the Governor's orders had been obtained.

Howard's vanity jumped with his inclination. He consented to the plot. A more ill-timed, idiotic maneuver, with the existing state of the public mind, it would be impossible to imagine. Either we must consider Terry and Howard weak-minded to the point of an inability to reason from cause to effect, or we must ascribe to them more sinister motives.

By now the Law and Order forces had become numerically more formidable.

The lower element flocked to the colors through sheer fright. A certain proportion of the organized remained in the ranks, though a majority had resigned. There was, as is usual in a new community, a very large contingent of wild, reckless young men without a care in the world, with no possible interest in the rights and wrongs of the case, or, indeed, in themselves. They were eager only for adventure and offered themselves just as soon as the prospects for a real fight seemed good. Then, too, they could always count on the five hundred Texans who had been imported.

There were plenty of weapons with which to arm these partisans. Contrary to all expectations, the Vigilance Committee had scrupulously refrained from interfering with the state armories. All the muskets belonging to the militia were in the armories and were available in different parts of the city. In addition, the State, as a commonwealth, had a right to a certain number of federal weapons stored in arsenals at Benicia. These could be requisitioned in due form.

But at this point, it has been said, the legal minds of the party conceived a bright plan. The muskets at Benicia on being requisitioned would have to cross the bay in a vessel of some sort Until the muskets were actually delivered they were federal property. Now if the Vigilance Committee were to confiscate the arms while on the transporting vessel, and while still federal property, the act would be piracy; the interceptors, pirates. The Law and Order people could legally call on the federal forces, which would be compelled to respond. If the Committee of Vigilance did not fall into this trap, then the Law and Order people would have the muskets anyway. [Mr. H.H. Bancroft, in his *Popular Tribunals*, holds that no proof of this plot exists.]

To carry out this plot they called in a saturnine, lank, drunken individual whose name was Hube Maloney.

Maloney picked out two men of his own type as assistants. He stipulated only that plenty of "refreshments" should be supplied. According to instructions Maloney was to operate boldly and flagrantly in full daylight. But the refreshment idea had been rather liberally interpreted. By six o'clock Rube had just sense enough left to anchor off Pueblo Point. There all gave serious attention to the rest of the refreshments, and finally rolled over to sleep off the effects.

In the meantime news of the intended shipment had reached the headquarters of the Vigilantes.

The Executive Committee went into immediate session. It was evident that the proposed disbanding would have to be postponed. A discussion followed as to methods of procedure to meet this new crisis. The Committee fell into the trap prepared for it. Probably no one realized the legal status of the muskets, but supposed them to belong already to the State.

Marshal Doane was instructed to capture them. He called to him the chief of the harbor police. "Have you a small vessel ready for immediate service?" he asked this man.

"Yes, a sloop, at the foot of this street."

"Be ready to sail in half an hour."

Doane then called to his assistance a quick-witted man named John Durkee. This man had been a member of the regular city police until the shooting of James King of William. At that time he had resigned his position and joined the Vigilance police. He was loyal by nature, steady in execution, and essentially quick-witted, qualities that stood everybody in very good stead as will be shortly seen. He picked out twelve reliable men to assist him, and set sail in the sloop.

For some hours he beat against the wind and the tide; but finally these became so strong that he was forced to anchor in San Pablo Bay until conditions had modified. Late in the afternoon he was again able to get under way.

Several of the tramps sailing about the bay were overhauled and examined, but none proved to be the prize. About dark the breeze died, leaving the little sloop barely under steerageway. A less persistent man than Durkee would have anchored for the night, but Durkee had received his instructions and intended to find the other sloop, and it was he himself who first caught the loom of a shadow under Pueblo Point.

He bore down and perceived it to be the sloop whose discovery he desired. The twelve men boarded with a rush, but found themselves in possession of an empty deck. The fumes of alcohol and the sound of snoring guided the boarding-party to the object of their search and the scene of their easy victory. Durkee transferred the muskets and prisoners to his own craft; and returned to the California Street wharf shortly after daylight. A messenger was dispatched to headquarters. He returned with instructions to deliver the muskets but to turn loose the prisoners. Durkee was somewhat astonished at the latter order but complied.

"All right," he is reported to have said. "Now, you measly hounds, you've got just about twenty-eight seconds to make yourselves as scarce as your virtues."

Maloney and his crew wasted few of the twenty-eight seconds in starting, but once out of sight they regained much of their bravado. A few drinks restored them to normal, and enabled them to put a good face on the report they now made to their employers. Maloney and his friends then visited in turn all the saloons. The drunker they grew, the louder they talked, reviling the Committee collectively and singly, bragging that they would shoot at sight Coleman, Truett, Durkee, and several others whom they named. They flourished weapons publicly, and otherwise became obstreperous. The Committee decided that their influence was bad and instructed Sterling Hopkins, with four others, to arrest the lot and bring them in.

The news of this determination reached the offending parties. They immediately fled to their masters like cur dogs. Their masters, who included Terry, Bowie, and a few others, happened to be discussing the situation in the office of Richard Ashe, a Texan. The crew burst into this gathering very much scared, with a statement that a "thousand stranglers" were at their heels. Hopkins, having left his small posse at the foot of the stairs, knocked and entered the room. He was faced by the muzzles of half a dozen pistols and told to get out of there.

Hopkins promptly obeyed.

If Terry had possessed the slightest degree of leadership he would have seen that this was the worst of all moments to precipitate a crisis. The forces of his own party were neither armed nor ready. But here, as in all other important crises of his career, he was governed by the haughty and headstrong passion of the moment.

Hopkins left his men on guard at the foot of the stairs, borrowed a horse from a passer-by, and galloped to headquarters. There he was instructed to return and stay on watch, and was told that reinforcements would soon follow. He arrived before the building in which Ashe's office was located in time to see Maloney, Terry, Ashe, McNabb, Bowie, and Howe, all armed with shot-guns, just turning a far corner. He dismounted and called on his men, who followed. The little posse dogged the judge's party for some distance. For a little time no attention was paid to them. But as they pressed closer, Terry, Ashe, and Maloney turned and presented their shot-guns. This was probably intended only as a threat, but Hopkins, who was always overbold, lunged at Maloney. Terry thrust his gun at a Vigilante who seized it by the barrel. At the same instant Ashe pressed the muzzle of his weapon against the breast of a man named Bovee, but hesitated to pull the trigger. It was not at that time as safe to shoot men in the open street as it had been formerly. Barry covered Rowe with a pistol. Rowe dropped his gun and ran towards the armory. The accidental discharge of a pistol seemed to unnerve Terry. He whipped out a long knife and plunged it into Hopkins's neck. Hopkins relaxed his hold on Terry's shot-gun and staggered back.

"I am stabbed! Take them, Vigilantes!" he said. He dropped to the sidewalk.

Terry and his friends ran towards the armory. Of the Vigilante posse only Bovee and Barry remained, but these two pursued the fleeing Law and Order men to the very doors of the armory itself. When the portals were slammed in their faces they took up their stand outside; and alone these two men held imprisoned several hundred men! During the next few minutes several men attempted entrance to the armory, among them our old friend Volney Howard. All were turned back and were given the impression that the armory was already in charge, of the Vigilantes. After a little, however, doubtless to the great relief of the "outside garrison" of the armory, the great Vigilante bell began to boom out its signals: *one, two, three—* rest; *one, two, three—*rest; and so on.

Instantly the streets were alive with men. Merchants left their customers, clerks their books, mechanics their tools. Draymen stripped their horses of harness, abandoned their wagons, and rode away to join their cavalry. Within an incredibly brief space of time everybody was off for the armory, the military companies marching like veterans, the artillery rumbling over the pavement. The cavalry, jogging along at a slow trot, covered the rear. A huge and roaring mob accompanied them, followed them, raced up the side-streets to arrive at the armory at the same time as the first files of the military force. They found the square before the building entirely deserted except for the dauntless Barry and Bovee, who still marched up and down singlehanded, holding the garrison within. They were able to report that no one had either entered or left the armory.

Inside the building the spirit had become one of stubborn sullenness. Terry was very sorry—as, indeed, he well might be—a Judge of the Supreme Court, who had no business being in San Francisco at all. Sworn to uphold the law, and ostensibly on the side of the Law and Order party, he had stepped out from his jurisdiction to commit as lawless and as idiotic a deed of passion and prejudice as could well have been imagined. Whatever chances the Law and Order party might have had heretofore were thereby dissipated. Their troops were scattered in small units; their rank and file had disappeared no one knew where; their enemies were fully organized and had been mustered by the alarm bell to their usual alertness and capability; and Terry's was the hand that had struck the bell!

He was reported as much chagrined. "This is very unfortunate, very unfortunate," he said; "but you shall not imperil *your* *l*ives for me. It is *I* they want. I will surrender to them."

Instead of the prompt expostulations which he probably expected, a dead silence greeted these words.

"There is nothing else to do," agreed Ashe at last.

An exchange of notes in military fashion followed. Ashe, as commander of the armory and leader of the besieged party, offered to surrender to the Executive Committee of the Vigilantes if protected from violence. The Executive Committee demanded the surrender of Terry, Maloney, and Philips, as well as of all arms and ammunition, promising that Terry and Maloney should be protected against persons outside the organization. On receiving this assurance, Ashe threw open the doors of the armory and the Vigilantes marched in.

"All present were disarmed," writes Bancroft. "Terry and Maloney were taken charge of and the armory was quickly swept of its contents. Three hundred muskets and other munitions of war were carried out and placed on drays. Two carriages then drove up, in one of which was placed Maloney and in the other Terry. Both were attended by a strong escort, Olney forming round them with his Citizens' Guard, increased to a battalion. Then in triumph the Committee men, with their prisoners and plunder enclosed in a solid body of infantry and these again surrounded by cavalry, marched back to their rooms."

Nor was this all. Coleman, like a wise general, realizing that compromise was no longer possible, sent out his men to take possession of all the encampments of the Law and Order forces. The four big armories were cleaned out while smaller squads of men combed the city house by house for concealed arms. By midnight the job was done. The Vigilantes were in control of the situation.

Chapter Sixteen: The Triumph of the Vigilantes

Judge Terry was still a thorny problem to handle. After all, he was a Judge of the Supreme Court. At first his attitude was one of apparent humility, but as time went on he regained his arrogant attitude and from his cell issued defiances to his captors. He was aided and abetted by his high-spirited wife, and in many ways caused the members of the Committee a great deal of trouble. If Hopkins were to die, they could do no less than hang Terry in common consistency and justice. But they realized fully that in executing a Justice of the Supreme Court they would be wading into pretty deep water. The state and federal authorities were inclined to leave them alone and let them work out the manifestly desirable reform, but it might be that such an act would force official interference. As one member of the Committee expressed it, "They had gone gunning for ferrets and had coralled a grizzly."

Nevertheless Terry was indicted before the Committee on the following counts, a statement of which gives probably as good a bird's eye view of Terry as numerous pages of personal description:

Resisting with violence the officers of the Vigilance Committee while in the discharge of their duties.

Committing an assault with a deadly weapon with intent to kill Sterling A. Hopkins on June 21, 1856.

Various breaches of the peace and attacks upon citizens while in the discharge of their duties, specified as follows:

1. Resistance in 1853 to a writ of habeas corpus on account of which one Roach escaped from the custody of the law, and the infant heirs of the Sanchez family were defrauded of their rights.

2. An attack in 1853 on a citizen of Stockton named Evans.

3. An attack in 1853 on a citizen in San Francisco named Purdy.

4. An attack at a charter election on a citizen of Stockton named King.

5. An attack in the court house of Stockton on a citizen named Broadhouse.

Before Terry's case came to trial it was known that Hopkins was not fatally wounded. Terry's confidence immediately rose. Heretofore he had been somewhat, but not much, humbled. Now his haughty spirit blazed forth as strongly as ever. He was tried in due course, and was found guilty on the first charge and on one of the minor charges. On the accusation of assault with intent to kill, the Committee deliberated a few days, and ended by declaring him guilty of simple assault. He was discharged and told to leave the State. But, for some reason or other, the order was not enforced.

Undoubtedly he owed his discharge in this form to the evident fact that the Committee did not know what to do with him. Terry at once took the boat for Sacramento, where for some time he remained in comparative retirement. Later he emerged in his old role, and ended his life by being killed at the hands of an armed guard of Justice Stephen Field whom Terry assaulted without giving Field a chance to defend himself.

While these events were going forward, the Committee had convicted and hanged two other men, Hetherington and Brace. In both instances the charge was murder of the most dastardly kind. The trials were conducted with due regard to the forms of law and justice, and the men were executed in an orderly fashion. These executions would not be remarkable in any way, were it not for the fact that they rounded out the complete tale of executions by the Vigilance Committee. Four men only were hanged in all the time the Committee held its sway. Nevertheless the manner of the executions and the spirit that actuated all the officers of the organization sufficed to bring about a complete reformation in the administration of justice.

About this time also the danger began to manifest itself that some of the less conscientious and, indeed, less important members of the Committee might attempt through political means to make capital of their connections. A rule was passed that no member of the Committee of Vigilance should be allowed to hold political office. Shortly after this decision, William Rabe was suspended for "having attempted to introduce politics into this body and for attempting to overawe the Executive Committee."

After the execution of the two men mentioned, the interesting trial of Durkee for piracy, the settlement by purchase of certain private claims against city land, and the deportation of a number of undesirable citizens, the active work of the Committee was practically over. It held complete power and had also gained the confidence of probably nine-tenths of the population. Even some of the erstwhile members of the Law and Order party, who had adhered to the forms of legality through principle, had now either ceased opposition, or had come over openly to the side of the Committee. Another date of adjournment was decided upon.

The gunnybag barricades were taken down on the fourteenth of August. On the sixteenth, the rooms of the building were ordered thrown open to all members of the Committee, their friends, their families, for a grand reception on the following week. It was determined then not to disorganize but to adjourn *sine die*. The organization was still to be held, and the members were to keep themselves ready whenever the need should arise. But preparatory to adjournment it was decided to hold a grand military review on the eighteenth of August. This was to leave a final impression upon the public mind of the numbers and powder of the Committee.

The parade fulfilled its function admirably. The Grand Marshal and his staff led, followed by the President and the Military Commanding General with his staff. Then marched four companies of artillery with fifteen mounted cannon. In their rear was a float representing Fort Gunnybags with imitation cannon. Next came the Executive Committee mounted, riding three abreast; then cavalry companies and the medical staff, which consisted of some fifty physicians of the town. Representatives of the Vigilance Committee of 1851 followed in wagons with a banner; then four regiments of infantry, more cavalry, citizen guards, pistol men, Vigilante police. Over six thousand men were that day in line, all disciplined, all devoted, all actuated by the highest motives, and conscious of a job well done.

The public reception at Fort Gunnybags was also well attended. Every one was curious to see the interior arrangement. The principal entrance was from Sacramento Street and there was also a private passage from another street. The doorkeeper's box was prominently to the front where each one entering had to give the pass-word. He then proceeded up the stairs to the floor above. The first floor was the armory and drill-room. Around the sides were displayed the artillery harness, the flags, bulletin-boards, and all the smaller arms. On one side was a lunch stand where coffee and other refreshments were dispensed to those on guard. On the opposite side were offices for every conceivable activity. An immense emblematic eye painted on the southeast corner of the room glared down on each as he entered. The front of the second floor was also a guard-room, armory, and drilling floor. Here also was painted the eye of Vigilance, and here was exhibited the famous ballot-box whose sides could separate the good ballots from the bad ballots. Here also were the meeting-rooms for the executive Committee and a number of cells for the prisoners. The police-office displayed many handcuffs, tools of captured criminals, relics, clothing with bullet holes, ropes used for hanging, bowie-knives, burglar's tools, brass knuckles, and all the other curiosities peculiar to criminal activities. The third story of the building had become the armorer's shop, and the hospital. Eight or ten workmen were employed in the former and six to twenty cots were maintained in the latter. Above all, on the roof, supported by a strong scaffolding, hung the Monumental bell whose tolling summoned the Vigilantes when need arose.

Altogether the visitors must have been greatly impressed, not only with the strength of the organization, but also with the care used in preparing it for every emergency, the perfection of its discipline, and the completeness of its equipment. When the Committee of Vigilance of 1856 adjourned subject to further call, there must have been in most men's minds the feeling that such a call could not again arise for years to come.

Yet it was not so much the punishment meted out to evil-doers that measures the success of the Vigilante movement. Only four villains were hanged; not more than thirty were banished. But the effect was the same as though four hundred had been executed. It is significant that not less than eight hundred went into voluntary exile.

"What has become of your Vigilance Committee?" asked a stranger naïvely, some years later.

"Toll the bell, sir, and you'll see," was the reply. [Bancroft, *Popular Tribunals*, 11, 695].

-End-

Bibliographical Note

California has been fortunate in her historians. Every student of the history of the Pacific coast is indebted to the monumental work of Hubert H. Bancroft. Three titles concern the period of the Forty-niners:

The History of California, 7 vols. (1884-1890);

California Inter Pocula, 1848-56 (1888);

Popular Tribunals, 2 vols. (1887).

Second only to these volumes in general scope and superior in some respects is:

T.H. Hittell's *History of California*, 4 vols. (1885-1897). Two other general histories of smaller compass and covering limited periods are I.B. Richman's *California under Spain and Mexico, 1535-1847* (1911),and Josiah Royce's *California, 1846-1856* (1886). The former is a scholarly but rather arid book; the latter is an essay in interpretation rather than a narrative of events.

One of the chief sources of information about San Francisco in the days of the gold fever is *The Annals of San Francisco (1855)* by Soulé and others.

Contemporary accounts of California just before the American occupation are of varying value. One of the most widely read books is R.H. Dana's *Two Years before the Mast* (1840). The author spent parts of 1835 and 1836 in California. *The Personal Narrative of James O. Pattie* (1831) is an account of six years' travel amid almost incredible hardships from St. Louis to the Pacific and back through Mexico. W.H. Thomes's *On Land and Sea, or California in the Years 1843, '44, and '45* (1892) gives vivid pictures of old Mexican days. Two other books may be mentioned which furnish information of some value: *Alfred Robinson, Life in California* (1846) and Walter Colton, *Three Years in California* (1850).

Personal journals and narratives of the Forty-niners are numerous, but they must be used with caution. Their accuracy is frequently open to question. Among the more valuable may be mentioned

Delano's *Life on the Plains and among the Diggings* (1854);

W.G. Johnston's *Experience of a Forty-niner* (1849); T.T. Johnson's *Sights in the Gold Region and Scenes by the Way* (1849);

J.T. Brooks's *Four Months among the Gold-Finders* (1849);

E.G. Buffum's *Six Months in the Gold Mines* (1850) the author was a member of the "Stevenson Regiment";

James Delevan's *Notes on California and the Placers: How to get there and what to do afterwards* (1850); and W.R. Ryan's *Personal Adventures in Upper and Lower California,* in 1848-9 (1850).

Others who were not gold-seekers have left their impression of California in transition, such as Bayard Taylor in his *Eldorado*, 2 vols. (1850), and J.W. Harlan in his *California '46 to '88* (1888). The latter was a member of Frémont's battalion.

The horrors of the overland journey are told by Delano in the book already mentioned and by W.L. Manly, *Death Valley in '49* (1894).

The evolution of law and government in primitive mining communities is described in C.H. Shinn's *Mining Camps. A Study in American Frontier Government* (1885).

The duties of the border police are set forth with thrilling details by Horace Bell, *Reminiscences of a Ranger or Early Times in Southern California* (1881).

An authoritative work on the Mormons is W.A. Linn's *Story of the Mormons* (1902).

For further bibliographical references the reader is referred to the articles on *California, San Francisco, The Mormons, and Frémont,* in The Encyclopaedia Britannica, 11th Edition.

* * * * * *

About Linda Pendleton

Linda Pendleton has written in a variety of genres: nonfiction, mystery novels, comic book scripting, and screenplays. She also coauthored nonfiction and fiction with her late husband, renowned author, Don Pendleton.

A native Californian, Linda is a member of The Authors Guild, and The Authors League, EPIC Authors, and Sisters in Crime. She was an EPIC Award Finalist in 2001 in the Thriller Category for the Novel, *Roulette* (previous title, *One Dark and Stormy Night*), and in 2002 was a finalist in the EPIC Nonfiction Philosophy Category for *Three Principles of Angelic Wisdom*. Her novel, *Shattered Lens: Catherine Winter, Private Investigator* is an EPIC 2011 Finalist, and *To Dance With Angels* by Don and Linda Pendleton is a 2012 EPIC Finalist. Although most of her time is devoted to her love of writing, she also enjoys the exploration of her family's genealogical roots.

Her website: www.lindapendleton.com

If you enjoyed this book and would like to read more about the California Gold Rush try Linda Pendleton's Kindle editions:

Gold, A Story of the California Gold Rush by Stewart Edward White with Introduction by Linda Pendleton.

The Forty-niners: The California Gold Rush by Stewart Edward White with Introduction by Linda Pendleton (Also Print).

Gold Hunters of Early California: Thomas Farish's Reminisces of the Gold Rush Days, Introduction by Linda Pendleton (Also Print)

Sierra Nevada Gold, 1849 by Linda Pendleton

Gold Rush: Three Years in California. Borthwick, Introduction by Linda Pendleton (Also Print)

And for More California History:

The Mountains, The Adventures of a Tenderfoot by Stewart Edward White with Introduction by Linda Pendleton.

Missions of California, William Henry Hudson, 1901, with Introduction by Linda Pendleton.

Legends of Southern California and San Francisco by George W. Caldwell, with Introduction by Linda Pendleton

United States History:

The Anti-Slavery Crusade: A Chronicle of the Gathering Storm of the 1800s by James Macy, with Introduction by Linda Pendleton.

CPSIA information can be obtained at www.ICGtesting.com
Printed in the USA
LVOW06s0531041213

363735LV00001B/54/P